SHAKESPEARE

III

1599-1604

GARETH LLOYD EVANS

OLIVER AND BOYD

EDINBURGH

OLIVER AND BOYD

Tweeddale Court
14 High Street,
Edinburgh EH1 1YL
(A division of Longman Group Limited)

0 05 002324 1 Hardback

0 05 002323 3 Paperback

Printed in Great Britain for Oliver and Boyd
by Cox & Wyman Ltd, London, Fakenham
and Reading

CONTENTS

PREFACE · · · vii

1 SHAKESPEARE AND THE GLOBE · · · 1

2 THE MATURE COMEDIES · · · 16
   Much Ado About Nothing · · · 16
   As You Like It · · · 27
   Twelfth Night · · · 38

3 THE "PROBLEM" PLAYS · · · 56
   All's Well That Ends Well · · · 62
   Measure for Measure · · · 74
   Troilus and Cressida · · · 84

4 ROME AND JULIUS CAESAR · · · 99

REFERENCES · · · 115

PREFACE

The first two volumes of this series were concerned with Shakespeare's life and works up to the time when he became firmly established as a leading dramatist in London. The present volume discusses the period of his early association with the Globe Theatre, which began in 1599. At this time he was writing some of the most optimistic and pessimistic works in the history of English drama—*As You Like It* and *Troilus and Cressida* alone are sufficient testimony to this. Yet apart from these he wrote *Twelfth Night*, *Much Ado About Nothing*, *All's Well That Ends Well*, *Measure for Measure*, very probably *Julius Caesar* and, almost certainly, *Hamlet* (which will be discussed in volume IV of this series). From 1599 until roughly the mid-point in the first decade of the seventeenth-century Shakespeare was at his most fecund as a dramatist —his imagination and confident dramatic skill seemed to gain sustenance from one another. It is from this time in his working life that one can truly say he was both complete poet and complete dramatist.

This book, like its predecessors, discusses Shakespeare's life in a given time-period and offers critical comment on those plays written during, or very close to, that period. It attempts to fuse academic speculation with theatrical experience. Students and playgoers will find that it devotes equal attention both to the plays as texts on the page with their inherent "dramatic" qualities as they are revealed in language, characterisation, language and construction, and to their "theatrical" reality as it is made manifest in performance.

The references to each chapter incorporate a specific bibliography for each volume. A larger and more comprehensive bibliography will appear in volume v. Bracketed page numbers have been inserted at the top of each inner margin to help the reader correlate text and references. The numbers on text pages denote the relevant pages of references and *vice versa*.

The Folio text of 1623 has been accepted as authoritative for *As You Like It, Twelfth Night, Julius Caesar, All's Well That Ends Well* and *Measure for Measure*, though in the last two cases the text is not a good one. The Quarto of 1600 (from which the Folio version was presumably taken) provides the text for *Much Ado About Nothing*.

Troilus and Cressida is a special problem; the Folio text was partly based on a 1609 Quarto and partly on Shakespeare's original manuscript. The Quarto is, on the whole, superior to the Folio text but omits both the Prologue and some forty-five lines of dialogue. Modern editors make a judicious selection from both Quarto and Folio and the old-spelling version used in this book is similarly eclectic.

So far as is possible the original punctuation of the chosen text has been retained, but in certain cases where it is unclear to the modern eye it has been changed to conform with modern usage. To facilitate reference to a modern edition, act, scene, and line references for quotations are given in square brackets from Peter Alexander's one-volume edition of the plays.

In all quotations the original spelling is left substantially unmodernised though the following alterations have been made silently: short "s" is used for long "s", and "i/j", "u/v", and "w/vv" are normalised. Common Elizabethan abbreviations like y^r for "your" and ñ for "nn" are expanded in full, as are ampersands.

The final stages of the preparation of this book were undertaken while I was in the United States and my wife contributed a great deal to ensuring its delivery for publication. I owe her a tremendous debt of gratitude. I should also like to thank Mr Jeremy Steele of Oliver and Boyd whose witty exactitude as an editor is greatly valued.

GARETH LLOYD EVANS

Stratford-upon-Avon 1971

I

SHAKESPEARE AND THE GLOBE

In the popular imagination Shakespeare's name has long been associated with the Globe Theatre, and the linking of the two names has been partially responsible for the maintenance of a romantic image of the dramatist. There is no more persistent theme in the romantic lore attached to Shakespeare than the vision of his striding out from a hard night's creating in his garret to meet his fellows for a drink, a talk, and argument, followed by rehearsal in a round theatre on Bankside. If the words Mermaid Tavern are added, the romantic picture is complete. Shakespeare is seen as an honoured member of a goodly fellowship, taking its work seriously, its pleasures heartily, and acquiring just enough rakishness from its profession's reputation to give romance a piquant sauce. Countless illustrations in expendable nineteenth-century editions of the plays have perpetuated the image, and Walter Bagehot is only one of many writers—distinguished and undistinguished—who have expressed it in words, conjuring up the dramatist:

> . . . now in fanciful solitude, now in cheerful solitude; now occupied with deep thoughts, now, and equally so, with trivial recreations, forgetting the dramatist in the man of substance, and the poet in the happy companion; beloved and even respected, with a hope for everyone and a smile for all.[1]

How true to reality this evocation is or, indeed, how guileless the real life of a theatre-man was, we do not know, though we have

cogent cause to doubt when we read of the harsh facts of the jungle
of the theatre-world in the 1590s. Where fancy and accuracy
agree, however, is in the substance of the fact that, for most of his
working life, Shakespeare was associated with one company, and
that this company's fame is inextricably linked with its occupancy
of the Globe Theatre from 1599 to 1608.[2] There is no certainty
about the company or companies to which Shakespeare be-
longed prior to 1594, but there is irrefutable evidence that he
joined the Lord Chamberlain's on or shortly after its formation in
1594.

By 1599 he was certainly living in London's theatre district on
Bankside, and there are indications that his move there from the
North Bank was not entirely dictated by the need to be near his
job:

> Eventually the collectors found that he had moved across
> the river to the London suburb on the Bankside. His name
> was accordingly transferred to the jurisdiction of the Liberty
> of the Clink, where the tax was eventually collected.[3]

At this time he seems to have had a few brushes with tax officials
and, indeed, with the law. An entry in the Controllment Rolls of
the Court of Queen's Bench for a surety of the peace may be
translated from its Latin original as follows:

> Be it known that William Wayte craves sureties of the peace
> against William Shakspare, Francis Langley, Dorothy Soer,
> wife of John Soer, and Anne Lee, for fear of death, and so
> forth.[4]

These evidences raise, a little wryly, ghosts of the litigious difficulties which had dogged his own father a decade or so earlier. In the
son's case there was a happier outcome.

By 1593 two companies dominated the London theatre—the
Lord Admiral's and Strange's Men (Lord Derby's) who worked in
collaboration. In the summer of 1594 a small group consisting of
Will Kempe, John Hemminge, Augustine Phillips, George
Bryan, Richard Cowley and Thomas Pope left Strange's Men and,
under the patronage of Lord Hunsdon, formed a new company

which took its name from Hunsdon's official post and became the Lord Chamberlain's Men.

In 1594 the company was performing at The Theatre, in Shore-ditch on the North Bank, which was managed by James Burbage. The first official record concerning it is found in the Chamber Accounts of 15 Mar. 1595, when Shakespeare, Will Kempe, and Burbage's son, Richard, were recorded as having received payments for two performances at Greenwich Palace in December 1594. This is strong confirmation that, by this date, Shakespeare had become a sharer in the company. The payment amounted to £20, and is referred to in these words:

> To Will[iam] Kempe Will[iam] Shakespeare & Richarde
> Burbage servantes to the Lord Chamb[er]leyne upon the
> councelles warr[ant] dated at Whitehall xv^{to} Martii 1594
> [1595 in the modern calendar] for twoe severall comedies or
> Enterludes shewed by them before her Ma[jesty] in [Christ]-
> mas tyme laste paste viz upon St Stephens daye &
> Innocentes daye xiij^l vj^s viij^d and by waye of her
> ma[jesty's] Rewarde vj^l xiij^{s}iiij^d in all xx^l.[5]

This single document contains three of the most famous names in the history of the British theatre. Richard Burbage came later to share with Edward Alleyn the status of leading tragic actor of the Elizabethan stage—they were the Gielgud and Olivier of their times. Alleyn specialised in playing the heroic characters of Marlowe; the parts through which Burbage was to shine were, in 1594, still to be written—Hamlet, Othello, Lear, Macbeth. His relationship with Shakespeare seems to have been based on more than professional closeness. In his will Shakespeare left Burbage 28/6d to buy a ring, and in 1613 they were both involved in designing and painting a shield for the Duke of Rutland.

Will Kempe was one of the most versatile comic actors of the time. He, like Shakespeare, joined the Lord Chamberlain's after a career which included touring in the provinces. He played Peter in *Romeo and Juliet* and Dogberry in *Much Ado*. Kempe was an eccentric, extrovert, physical comedian—one guesses that his style of acting is best reflected in the silent-film antics of the Keystone

Cops. In 1599, after he had sold his shares in the Globe Theatre, he spent a month dancing from London to Norwich. He was, by all accounts, a fine juggler and dancer, but he was a restless man. After his Norwich feat he wandered in Italy and Germany; by 1602 he had joined Worcester's company; it is conjectured that by 1608 he was dead.

The company played at all sorts of venues—at The Theatre (the first professional, commercial London building), in inn yards, at court, and in many *ad hoc* auditoriums in the provinces. If it can be said to have had a London home, then this, in the early days, was The Theatre. The land on which it stood had been leased to James Burbage by Giles Allen in April 1576. The lease was for twenty-one years at an annual rent of £14. By 1596 Burbage had quarrelled with the landowner about the renewal of the lease, but he died in the following year. His son, Cuthbert Burbage, who had inherited the lease decided, in December 1598, to pull down the building. On 20 Jan. 1599 the timber and other materials of the fabric were transferred to another site on the South Bank. Peter Street

> and divers other persons, to the number of twelve . . .
> armed themselves . . . and throwing downe the sayd Theater
> in verye outragious, violent and riotous sort . . . did then
> alsoe in most forcible and ryotous manner take and carrye
> awaye from thence all the wood and timber thereof unto the
> Banckesyde in the parishe of St Marye Overyes, and there
> erected a newe playhowse with the sayd timber and woode.[6]

Peter Street was in charge of the operation. The site for the "newe playhowse" was owned by Nicholas Brend, who leased it for £14 10. 0. a year rental on a thirty-one-year lease. This lease was conveyed in two halves: one half to the Burbage brothers, Cuthbert and Richard; the other, divided into five equal parts, to Shakespeare, Hemminge, Phillips, Pope, and Will Kempe. The commitment of the dramatist to the Lord Chamberlain's Men and to the Globe Theatre was complete. It was undoubtedly one of the most important combinations of talent in the history of art.

It would be of value to know the extent of Shakespeare's financial involvement in these transactions, so that a measure could be taken of his financial status at this time. With customary disguise, however, the records do not enable us to do more than guess that he would not have been asked to join the consortium unless he had visible means—although it must be remembered that, as dramatist, Shakespeare represented tremendous potential assets. The general purpose of his involvement, and the responsibilities entailed, emerge from a document of 1635. The survivors of the Burbage family replied to a petition drawn up by members of the company which aimed at getting the ownership of the shares more widely spread among them. It reads:

> The father of us Cutbert & Rich[ard] Burbage was the first builder of Playhowses & was himselfe in his younger yeeres a Player. The Theater hee built w[ith] many Hundred poundes taken up at interest. The Players that lived in those first times had onely the profitts arising from the dores, but now the players receave all the commings in at the dores to them selves & halfe the Galleries from the Housekeepers. Hee [i.e. James Burbage] . . . had a great suite in law & by his death, the like troubles fell on us, his sonnes; wee then bethought us of altering from thence, & at like expence built the Globe w[ith] more summes of money taken up at interest, which lay heavy on us many yeeres, & to o[ur]selves wee joined those deserving men, Shakspere Hemings, Condall, Philips and others partners in [the] profittes of that they call the House.[7]

This document, though tantalisingly vague, gives a vivid evocation of the problems which beset the Burbage family—Shakespeare, without doubt, was heavily involved in the triumphs and vicissitudes.

Shakespeare's administrative position in the Lord Chamberlain's company and in the Globe was, therefore, at the very centre of the activities. Yet it is his artistic involvement which warms the imagination. The common view that he wrote all of his plays for first performance at the Globe is of course incorrect and, ironically enough, the play most often associated, in the imagination, with this theatre (*Henry V*) may well have been written and produced before the completion of the new building in September 1599. Shakespeare, in fact, wrote no other history plays for first performance there, except *Henry VIII*, and two of his tragedies (*Titus Andronicus* and *Romeo and Juliet*) were written well before the opening.

A mixture of factual evidence and reasoned conjecture presents us with a pattern of Shakespeare's plays at the Globe. The most likely candidate for a first-night-ever Shakespeare production in the new theatre is *Julius Caesar*, of which there is a performance recorded for 21 Sept. 1599. As Bernard Beckermann says, "Several plays are on the borderline."

> *As You Like It, Much Ado About Nothing* and *Henry V* were "staid" from printing, according to the Stationers' Register entry of August 4, 1600. Since none of them appears in Meres' listing in 1598, they all fall within the two-year intervening period. In dating *As You Like It* and *Much Ado About Nothing* there is very little evidence for narrowing the period. The appearance of Kempe's name in speech prefixes in *Much Ado* (IV, ii) places it before the opening of the Globe. O. J. Campbell points out that *As You Like It* must have been written after the edict against satire on July 1, 1599. These facts, together with the general consensus, lead me to include *As You Like It* in the 1599–1608 repertory and to exclude *Much Ado*.[8]

In 1608 the close relationship between the Lord Chamberlain's Men and the Globe came to an end. They continued, intermittently, to perform there (as Forman's evidence proves)[9] but this date really marks the end of a great combination between an acting company and a specific theatre. In 1608, a bad plague year, the theatres were closed from July to December. In August of that year some of the shares in the Blackfriars Theatre belonging to Cuthbert and Richard Burbage were distributed among the company—to Shakespeare, Hemminge, Condell and Sly. In late 1609, after having to tour because of the plague, the Lord Chamberlain's, or King's Men (as they had become known since the accession of James I) took over the Blackfriars Theatre. Some of Shakespeare's later plays were undoubtedly written for first performance at this new kind of theatre.

Even allowing for the uncertainties about the number of Shakespeare's plays first produced at the Globe, there can be no doubt that its audiences witnessed the first performances of some of the greatest artistic works of man, both in comedy and tragedy. Its leading actor—Richard Burbage—has the unique distinction of having been the first man to have realised and embodied Hamlet, Othello, Lear, and Macbeth on its stage. Its great comic actor, Robert Armin, certainly played Feste there and perhaps Lear's Fool, and a handful of unknown men and boys brought to theatrical life for the first time the parts of Viola, Orsino, Angelo, Isabella, Claudius, Gertrude, Desdemona, Iago and many others.

Yet there is more to be recorded. On the stage of this Globe Theatre were seen Ben Jonson's *Every Man Out of his Humour*, *Sejanus* and *Volpone*.[10] Another great and, until the Royal Shakespeare Company blew the dust away from it, an unjustifiably neglected play, probably had its first performance at the Globe—*The Revenger's Tragedy*.[11]

The record of first performances is, in itself, formidable, but one must add to it the implication of the facts that the population of London at the turn of the sixteenth century was certainly no more than one hundred thousand, and probably nearer fifty thousand, and that the capacity of the Globe was in the region of two thousand. For most of its life the theatre flourished, and so it is obvious that the percentage of the population which saw plays there was very high—much higher than today's London theatre-going population. Indeed, in the face of such a record, imagination may be excused for indulging in excited fancies about this theatre and its relationship to the great art of its time.

The way in which this theatre and the company which inhabited it seemed to serve as a magnet to genius and talent should not be allowed to make us forget that intensity of artistic imagination and skill almost inevitably leads to rivalry, jealousy, envy. The Globe was the golden centre of drama, but it was involved in one of the most spectacular, acrimonious and, in many ways, baffling literary quarrels of all time. Ironically, while the quarrel produced the worst in terms of a venting of personal spleen, it also produced the best in terms of a number of superbly executed satirical pieces. But, typically, while the evidence we have undoubtedly suggests Shakespeare's involvement, the extent of that involvement, as in the case of nearly all his life's activities, is shadowy, uncertain, intriguing.

There is no question but that Ben Jonson was a close associate of Shakespeare's.[12] Romantic image-making, such as is raised by Keats's *Lines on the Mermaid Tavern*,

> Souls of Poets dead and gone,
> What Elysium have ye known,
> Happy field or mossy cavern,
> Choicer than the Mermaid Tavern?

is posterity's wish to father a thought. But in the reality of close literary friendships the warm intimacy prompted by similar professional ambitions may be cooled by temperament, by rivalry of methods, and by the chances of public acclaim. Ben Jonson and Shakespeare were thrown into close relationship by the accidents of genius, time, and profession; and, when men of artistic sensibility are thus placed together, they often instinctively recognise what each considers to be the virtues and weaknesses of the other. Ben Jonson, it is certain, loved Shakespeare the man; his admiration for Shakespeare's genius was, however, tempered by qualifications.

In the relaxed mood when the demands of profession, the material world and personal obsessions are in abeyance, the very fact of knowing, or having known, a man whose imagination and skill are as a garland to one's own profession produces a warmth of affection. Thus Ben Jonson:

. . . I lov'd the man, and doe honour his memory (on this side Idolatry) as much as any.

There was ever more in him to be praysed, then to be pardoned.

Hee was (indeed) honest, and of an open, and free nature.

Those words of Jonson do, indeed, bespeak a sort of loving. Yet he was also a writer, one of the trade, and the very candour which prompted him to write such words, pushes him into a further, perhaps more particular, truth.

> I *remember*, the Players have often mentioned it as an honour to *Shakespeare*, that in his writing, (whatsoever he penn'd) hee never blotted out line. My answer hath beene. would he had blotted a thousand.
>
> . . . Shaksperr wanted Arte.
>
> . . . *thou hadst small* Latine, *and less* Greeke . . .
>
> His wit was in his owne power; would the rule of it had beene so too.[13]

There is, basically, no contradiction between these two sets of statements. They are both the result of candour; they are, one suspects, both true. Ben Jonson loved the man, admired the work, but deprecated the means. For him the limitations of Shakespeare's art were simply but cogently expressible:

> Though neede make many *Poets*, and some such
> As art, and nature have not betterd much;
> Yet ours, for want, hath not so lov'd the stage,
> As he dare serve th'ill customes of the age:
> Or purchase your delight at such a rate,
> As, for it, he himselfe must justly hate.
> To make a child, now swadled, to proceede
> Man, and then shoote up, in one beard, and weede,
> Past threescore yeeres: or, with three rustie swords,
> And helpe of some few foot-and-halfe-foote words,
> Fight over *Yorke*, and *Lancasters* long jarres:
> And in the tyring-house bring wounds, to scarres.[14]

Shakespeare's "wanting" is of an art governed by classical principles. For Jonson, Shakespeare's "wit" was too much in his own power. He would have agreed with his contemporary Sir Philip Sidney, who, in writing about Aristotle, spoke for all adherents of classical principles:

For it is faulty both in Place and Time, the two necessary
companions of all corporal actions. For where the stage
should always represent but one place, and the uttermost
time presupposed in it should be, both by *Aristotle*'s
precept and common reason, but one day: there is both
many days, and many places, inartificially imagined.[15]

Yet, in his milder moments, Jonson might perhaps have concurred
with Dryden: "If I would compare Jonson with Shakespeare, I
must acknowledge him the more correct poet, but Shakespeare
the greater wit."[16]

The conflict was between "natural" and "classical". The
friendship between them was, one suspects, likely at any time to
squall upon this matter. Thomas Fuller has, saving his fancy,
encompassed the situation well.

> Many were the *wit-combates* betwixt him and Ben Johnson
> [sic], which two I behold like a *Spanish great Gallion* and an
> *English man of war*; Master Johnson (like the former) was
> built Far higher in learning; *Solid*, but *slow* in his perfor-
> mances. *Shake-spear*, with the *English man of war*, lesser in
> bulk, but lighter in *sailing*, could turn with all tides, tack
> about and take advantage of all winds, by the quickness of
> his Wit and Invention.[17]

It was probably because of the irreconcilable nature of their
artistic imaginations that Shakespeare found himself caught in the
cross-winds of the great literary quarrel. The tempests which it
raised blew from many quarters; in part it was private feud, in
part a manifestation of rivalry between different theatres, in part
the result of opposing artistic principles.

In 1599 Marston's *Histriomastix* appeared with a character
(Chrisoganus) who was obviously, and not flatteringly, modelled
on Ben Jonson. The immediate reply was a parody of Marston's
overblown style in *Every Man Out of his Humour* and *Cynthia's
Revels*. Jonson seems to have been responsible for widening the
quarrel—in the latter play, for example, Dekker is castigated as
well as Marston. The two dramatists immediately planned a reply

to Jonson, but he discovered their intentions and, working at a pressure which was both uncongenial and unusual for him, produced *The Poetaster* in fifteen weeks. Marston received the main fury of the attack in this play; the most famous scene is one in which Horace (Jonson) forces Crispinus (Marston) to swallow a purge made up of his brain and bowels—this severe remedy enables him to vomit out many of the inflated and pretentious elements in his vocabulary. *The Poetaster* was performed by the children of Blackfriars in 1601.

Dekker and Marston's reply—*Satiromastix*—was performed by the children of St Paul's and, intriguingly enough, also at the Globe Theatre, by the Lord Chamberlain's company—one which had presented Jonson's own plays. The production seems to have marked the end of the most virulent part of the quarrel. It rambled on but, as is often the way of the literary profession, in 1605 Jonson and Marston collaborated in the writing of *Eastward Ho!*

The extent to which Shakespeare was blown about is not known, but we catch inklings of his being involved. It seems likely that he was not a leading participant, but a relatively innocent victim; indeed, as on other occasions when Shakespeare is mentioned (excepting Greene's famous attack)[18] there seems to have been a marked reluctance on the part of any of his colleagues to villify him or to damage his reputation. There is a very strong impression that throughout his life Shakespeare not only refused to become involved in faction in an obvious partisan way, but that he was generally respected for a gentle neutrality.

There is a possible reference to Shakespeare in some lines in the *Apologetical Dialogue* written by Jonson after the appearance of *Satiromastix* in 1601. After attempting to defend some of the attacks he has made, he writes:

> Onely amongst them, I am sorry for
> Some better natures, by the rest so drawne,
> To run in the vile line.

Shakespeare's connection with the quarrel is indicated more firmly by some lines in *The Second Parte of the Returne from Parnassus*,

(*3 Parnassus*), written in Cambridge in 1601–2. This was the third
of a trio of university dramas, typical in their plethora of topical
allusions, satirical sallies and self-conscious erudition. Two students
trying to become actors with the Lord Chamberlain's company are
interviewed by Kempe and Burbage, who subsequently discuss
them. Kempe says:

> Few of the university men pen plaies well, they smell too
> much of that writer *Ovid*, and that writer *Metamorphosis*,
> and talk too much of *Proserpina* & *Juppiter*. Why heres our
> fellow Shakespeare puts them all down, I and *Ben Jonson*
> too. O that *Ben Jonson* is a pestilent fellow, he brought up
> Horace by giving the Poets a pill, but our fellow *Shakespeare*
> hath given him a purge that made him beray his crèdit.

What was the "purge" that Shakespeare (obviously, here, the
darling of the non-classically minded Kempe) administered to
Ben Jonson? It has been suggested that Jonson is satirised in
Jaques, in Ajax, and in Nym. A very likely explanation is that the
purge was the *Satiromastix* itself. The writer of *Parnassus 3* may
have wrongly believed that Shakespeare wrote it—it must be
remembered that Kempe and Burbage are main characters, and
they were fellows of Shakespeare.

Whatever the missing elements in Shakespeare's involvement
might be, there can be little doubt that in 1599 he was regarded as
being a completely different kind of dramatist from Jonson. The
likelihood is that, willy-nilly, Shakespeare found himself regarded
as the chief and admired representative of the "natural" drama, that
he played little part in consciously putting himself forward as such,
and that even those, like Jonson, who cleaved to the classical principles, could not bring themselves to do more than gently admon-
ish the man whom Francis Meres, in his *Palladis Tamia* (1598), had
called "sweete" and "hony-tongued". In any case, from 1597 up to
the opening of the Globe Theatre, Shakespeare was too busily
engaged to involve himself too closely with anything that
deflected him from two particular purposes—the advancement of
his career as a dramatist and the increasing of his prosperity.

One of the most remarkable features of Shakespeare's life in

London during this most productive time in his career is that Stratford-upon-Avon seems never to have been very far away from his mind. The shrewd and careful countryman, watchful of his holdings, is manifest even in the scanty documents that we have. It is beyond reason to deny that he found occasion to visit his birthplace. It is likely that he was there in August 1596 on the melancholy occasion of the death and burial of his son Hamnet, and he may have been there in 1597 to conduct one of the most important business ventures of his life—the purchase of New Place. This, one of the largest houses in Stratford, had been built in the late fifteenth century by Sir Hugh Clopton. Its purchase was an affirmation of the prosperity which his dramatic work was rapidly attaining for him; perhaps too, it served as a salve for the disappointed and ageing John Shakespeare, who two decades before had stood upon the pinnacle of prosperity but had now fallen from that and from public status. The deed for the purchase was recorded on 4 May 1597.

> Inter Willielmum Shakespeare querentem et Willielmum Underhill generosum deforciantem de uno mesuagio duobus horreis et duobus gardinis cum pertinenciis in Stratford super Avon.[19]

Shakespeare wasted little time in making New Place into a living, thriving home. By February 1598 he had begun to store grain on the property:

> Stratforde Burrowghe, Warrwicke. The noate of corne & malte Taken the iiij of ffebruarij 1597 in the XLth yeare of the raigne of our moste gracious Soveraigne Ladie Queen Elizabethe etc. . . . . Chapple street Warde. . . . W[m]. Shackspere. X quarters.[20]

It is more than possible that John Shakespeare had played some part in ensuring that his son stored what was, at the time, a considerable amount of grain. John Shakespeare would have known that the three unusually wet summers of 1594, 1595, and 1596 had seriously affected the grain harvest. Indeed, his part of Warwickshire was worst hit. The Privy Council had tried to prevent the hoarding of grain by reminding J.P.s of a set of orders made against it in 1586. The discontent and unrest among country people, because of hoarding and profiteering, did not prevent the Shakespeare family from stocking the thirteenth largest amount of grain in the Stratford borough.

It is reasonable to suppose that the purchase of New Place and its setting-up as a large and prosperous home required Shakespeare's presence at Stratford. His connections with the town were also maintained by correspondence. With a characteristic meanness where Shakespeare is concerned, history has left us with examples of letters written *to* him, but none of his replies. There must have been many, concerned with the expansion of his business and property interests in and about Stratford.

On 24 Jan. 1598 Abraham Sturley wrote to his friend Richard Quiney, then visiting London, suggesting that he get in touch with Shakespeare about land near Shottery and also about the heavy Stratford taxes:

> It semeth by him [Quiney's father] that our countriman, Mr Shaksper, is willinge to disburse some monei upon some od yardeland or other att Shottri or neare about us; he thinketh it a very fitt patterne to move him to deale in the matter of our tithes.[21]

Whatever the result was, nine months later Richard Quiney was addressing Shakespeare in very warm and respectful terms. He was again in London and wrote to Shakespeare for a loan of £30 to pay his London debts—Master Quiney seems to have been no laggard in his desire to visit the capital or to spend a very large sum of money there. "To my Loveinge good ffrend & contreymann Mr Wm. Shackespere deliver thees", he begins; and continues:

> Loveinge Contreyman, I am bolde of yowe as of a ffrende, craveinge yowre helpe with XXXli uppon Mr Bushells & my securytee or Mr Myttons with me . . . Yowe shall ffrende me muche in helpeinge me out of all the debettes I owe in London, I thancke god, & muche quiet my mynde which wolde nott be indebeted. . . .[22]

In short, Richard Quiney was in a mess. Whether he considered

Shakespeare to be a "soft touch", or whether sheer desperation drove him to write the letter, we cannot tell. It seems unlikely that Shakespeare would have been easily swayed—the record of his shrewdness and care is too definite for that. Yet, careful as he was, Shakespeare was apparently a fair and generous man—his will suggests this.

The opening of the Globe, his rise in fame, the growth of his prosperity, his interests in Stratford, large as they are in what they tell us of his activities, pale by the side of the imaginative and intellectual activity proven by the plays that he wrote in the latter part of the 1590s. When we contemplate those written around the time when the Lord Chamberlain's company was coming to dominate the theatre-world, just prior to the opening of the Globe, we may imagine that the excitement of the times, the growing maturity of art and skill, are expressing themselves with tremendous happy affirmation. *Henry V*, *As You Like It*, *Much Ado*, *Twelfth Night* seem to represent Shakespeare in his most optimistic mood.

These affirming plays are, perhaps, the spontaneous reaction to feelings of goodwill, imaginative assurance, material stability. They are, perhaps, a kind of thank-offering to fortune which had begun to smile. Yet it is a great mistake to assume that the great artist has a simple response to this kind of fortune. The old, clock-work, view of Shakespeare entering a "comic" period, only to suffer some hazard of fate, and to respond by entering into a "problem" period, passing thence by degrees to a "tragic" period, is negatived by the very nature of these plays that, as a generalisation, we call "happy" and "affirmative".

None of the plays of the late 1590s which are designated as "comedies" are simply effusions of joy. The balance of forces is, for the moment, tipped in the direction of comedy and affirmation. Yet there is enough in their characters and themes to suggest that, thank-offerings though they may be, in a sort, they are inextricably part of a complex, deepening vision of the world, which had begun to find expression a decade before, and which was to develop and embody itself in very disturbing ways over the next few years.

2

THE MATURE COMEDIES
Much Ado About Nothing

The least satisfying and least gracious part of *Much Ado About Nothing* is the plot involving Claudio and Hero—which Shakespeare took from an earlier story. What affords us most delight are the Beatrice/Benedick episodes—Shakespeare's own invention. The first plot was most probably found in his reading of an Italian *novella* by Bandello, though a version of it occurs in Ariosto's *Orlando Furioso*.[1] The rest, including Dogberry and Verges, comes from the chambers of his own imagination. It is no mere academic exercise to distinguish the geneses of the two plots because, in fact, the differences between them in terms of emotional atmosphere, characterisation and spirit can create serious problems for our acceptance of the play as an entity. Claudio seems priggish, mentally underdeveloped, self-indulgent, and, in the end, reaps a reward which seems flattering to his deserts. Hero, though wronged and victimised, never completely conquers our affections. She is (if we are honest to our experience of the play) a somewhat faint and fainting maiden suitable for inclusion among the wilting heroines of nineteenth-century melodrama. She lacks that brave spirit whose possession would make her presence poignant rather than, as it is, irritating. Juliet is as much wronged as Hero, but she gains our admiration and pity because of her strength of will and spirit. Shakespeare has given Hero little will and spirit; she is a mechanism in a plot which, by itself, is curiously tasteless in its absurdity. There is no gainsaying, however, that this is a twentieth-century judgement. The nineteenth century, and perhaps the sixteenth, would have found Hero pathetically heroic, and

Claudio, if a shade misguided, eventually to be praised for doing his manly duty like a man.

By contrast, the Beatrice/Benedick story has a fresh, acidic quality, sweetened by its conclusion, and made especially palatable by the tartly clever wit which characterises their relationship. These two are no less under the spell of illusion than is Claudio or, for that matter, the rest of the characters, but we have a lingering feeling that they are half-aware of it; sustaining it to the end seems, in them, part of a game they are prepared to enjoy. Like Kate and Petruchio they ride upon illusion like happy ships, confidently discovering where their harbour lies.

Regarded separately and superficially, the two plots are incompatible, both in their quality and in their effects upon the audience. The one tends to drive us away from the play, the other seems to invite us in.

It is all the more remarkable, therefore, that the play is among the popular favourites of audiences and that, in good performance, it seems to have a quality of firm unity and balanced construction. In the words of the Arden editor, "Perhaps of all the plays this comedy gains most by representation on the stage and loses least."[2] The reasons for its success on-stage are many but the decisive variety of its moods would seem to be one of the most important. The first two scenes have a gamesome, almost festive atmosphere, reminiscent of the early comedies: warriors are returned from wars, ladies and celebrations await them. The scenes between Don John and his confidantes—Borachio and Conrade—have the half-absurd quality of bare-faced melodramatic villainy. The Dogberry/Verges scenes are superbly farcical. The garden scenes, in which Beatrice and Benedick are duped, have the artful shape, movement, and verbal dexterity of restoration comedy. The church scene takes us beyond unreal melodrama towards the edge of dark pathos. The conclusion, even if in our hearts we know it to be forced by the plot-mechanics, still satisfies that yearning, which never abates in audiences, to see (if not justice) at least theatrical logic.

Variety of this nature does not, of course, guarantee an overall unity—on the contrary it might very well deny the possibility. In this play, however, the variety that has been noted is given a cohesion held firm by strong dramatic and theatrical bonds. All the sub-episodes—like the Don John/Borachio/Conrade scenes and the Dogberry scenes—serve to guide the main direction of the play. The Claudio/Hero plot would be impossible without them; similarly, the working-out of the Beatrice/Benedick story would lack meaning without the results of the intrigue which is initiated by Don John and which Dogberry, like a lucky bassett hound with no sense of smell, eventually uncovers.

Again, the fact that the play is largely written in prose aids the credibility of the whole, and is an important factor in the element of contrast which characterises it. As Foakes has pointed out:

> . . . the characters whose speech is almost wholly in prose (Beatrice and Benedick; Dogberry and Verges) have more life and depth than those who speak verse most of the time (Claudio, Leonato, Antonio, Hero). In this play such a contrast seems natural, for like Berowne . . . Benedick and Beatrice deliberately reject
>> *Taffeta phrases, silken terms precise,*
>> *Three-piled hyperboles, spruce affectation,*
> in favour of witty prose . . .[3]

In short, it is correct wit which is held in tension with over-pretty sophistication in this play, and in the end the innate honesty and candour of the former overcomes the self-deception of the latter.

In the three mature comedies (*Much Ado*, *As You Like It* and *Twelfth Night*) written in close proximity, a young woman dominates our experience of each play and, by her presence, makes acceptable a series of events and characters which are, to say the least, unpalatable. Beatrice, Rosalind and Viola are the agencies through which the plays are finally edged into the status of happy, contented romantic comedy. Claudio's priggishness, Hero's ineffectiveness, Don John's perfidy, the hedonism of the court—all these are irritants to our sensibilities in much the same way as are Orsino's self-indulgence, Orlando's relative effeteness, the

Duke's accesses of anger. It is the romantic heroines who sweeten what is, in many ways, a bitter pill.

Something of the nature and dominance of Beatrice's character is given at her very first appearance in the action. Two matters are certain. The first is that he would be a brave person who was prepared to take her on in a battle of wits. Her taunting reference to Benedick bespeaks a tough spirit—one that has girded its loins for attack not defence.

> O Lord, he will hang upon him like a disease, hee is sooner
> caught than the pestilence, and the taker runs presently
> madde, God help the noble Claudio, if he have caught the
> Benedict, it will cost him a thousand pound ere a be cured.
> [I. i. 70–4]

The second is that Beatrice seems easy in the presence of men. She displays no wilting femininity, no suggestion of subservience either to men's whims and foibles or to any conventions of society that women should know their place. She speaks as an equal and, more to the point, she has to be accepted as an equal. Critical opinion which notes the strength of personality common to the three comic heroines has often failed to point out a peculiarity in Beatrice. It is that she is shown as more than holding her own in men's company without her will having to be shored up by disguise. When Viola and Rosalind revert to female dress they immediately take up the rôle of loved and loving, but dutiful spouses; disguise aids their determination to find love but, when it is dropped, they become man's willing mate. Beatrice has no such aid; the absence of disguise marks her off absolutely from the other two. She seems to be in a position of greater loneliness. Having, so to speak, established herself as the equal of men, she has to preserve that equality without the hope of any concession on their part to her femininity. She battles alone, and no one gives any quarter. Her loneliness is quite different from that of Viola's. The price she has to pay for being accepted as man's intellectual equal is, for a long time, to be misunderstood; the price Viola has to pay for her solitary harbouring of love for Orsino is to watch with anguish the possibility of his marrying another. It is the difference between willed and fated isolation. Beatrice has taken up an attitude towards Benedick which almost forces her to generalise it towards all men. She drives herself into a position where her determination to engage in nothing but verbal banter is giving her the reputation of being a manhater. She is "a professed tyrant to their sex" and it is said that she "cannot abide to hear tell of a husband". Yet, from time to time, the price paid for striking up this attitude is revealed in a curious strain of comic pathos.

> I have a good eie, unkle; I can see a church by day-light.
>
> [II. I. 69–70]
>
> Thus goes every one to the world but I, and I am sun-burnt, I may sit in a corner and crie Heigh ho for a husband.
>
> [II. I. 286–8]

It is, assuredly, all part of a kind of game, but the attractiveness of her character lies in the fact that within the game there is a serious and, at times, heart-catching truth. It may be expressed by noting that the nature of her personality forces her to play a game, to banter, to appear recklessly gay in her strictures on men and the idea of a husband; yet something else exists. Inside her a silent battle is going on.

She makes one very touching and precipitate exit from the action. She has bantered with Don Pedro about how she would marry his brother if he had one and he, mockingly, then offers himself. She replies:

> I would rather have one of your fathers getting: hath your grace ne'er a brother like you? your father got excellent husbands if a maide could come by them.

The prince's response is to remind her of what everybody expects from her,

> To be merry best becomes you, for out of question, you were borne in a merry hower.

She answers, as if to confirm the general view,

No sure my lord, my mother cried, but then there was a
starre daunst, and under that was I borne, cosins God give
you joy.

Leonato asks,

Neece, will you looke to those things I tolde you of.

and quickly she turns upon him and says,

I crie you mercy uncle, by your graces pardon.
[II. I. 299–307]

I have no doubt that she leaves the stage crying. For a moment the
battle between her "given" disposition and her own desires has
become too much for her. Moments like this teach us in the audience that there is more to Beatrice than dancing star, and when
they come they prepare us to accept the mood she displays in the
church scene with Benedick.

The first long scene between them is a dazzling battle of wit.

Ben. God keepe your hardiship stil in that mind, so some
    Gentleman or other shall escape a predestinate scratcht
    face.
Bea. Scratching could not make it worse, and twere such a
    face as yours were.
Ben. Well, you are a rare parratt teacher.
Bea. A bird of my tongue is better than a beast of yours.
Ben. I would my horse had the speed of your tongue, and
    so good a continuer, but keep your way a Gods name,
    I have done.
Bea. You always end with a jades trick, I knowe you of
    olde.
[I. I. 113–24]

The difference in the church scene is extraordinary.

Bea. I love you with so much of my heart, that none is left
    to protest.
Ben. Come bid me doe anything for thee.
Bea. Kill *Claudio.*

Ben. Ha, not for the wide world.

Bea. You kill me to deny it, farewell.

[IV. I. 284–9]

Benedick is, in the long run, a foil to Beatrice. We never feel that he will get the better of her in any witty exchange. His sallies, his rumbustiousness, seem less a result of willed determination than hers. Indeed what Don Pedro says of this side of the man is very near the truth:

He dooth indeede shew some sparkes that are like wit.

[II. III. 171]

When he is in Beatrice's presence his witty weapons do not seem so effectively cutting as when he is with others. There is something comparable, here, to the relationships between Rosalind and Orlando and Viola and Orsino. They seem lesser mortals in the presence of these women, however much they may seem to shine and show certain strengths and authorities in the presence of other people. Orsino's aristocratic and autocratic leadership of his court pales to nothing in the shadow of his curious ineffectiveness in the company of Viola; Orlando's physical courage is over-shadowed by his emotional subservience to Rosalind in the forest of Arden. In the final analysis, the difference between these three heroines and their male wooers is that the females are intellectually, morally, and emotionally, more mature than the males. The church scene in *Much Ado* confirms this. The true spirit of Beatrice is revealed—she is a woman of great fidelity to those she loves, of great moral determination, and entirely truthful. For the sake of the truth about Hero being revealed and the punishment of Claudio being achieved, she is prepared to stake all that her love for Benedick means. She can only love a man who can come near to matching her own intellectual resource, her fidelity, and her sense of what is true and what is false. She teaches him what is inside him, much as Rosalind teaches Orlando, and Viola Orsino, the meaning of true love. The Friar's words (though they are specifically directed at Claudio) sum up the truth of what happens to Benedick when he realises that to ensure Beatrice's love he must accept her standards.

That what we have, we prize not to the worth,
Whiles we enjoy it, but being lackt and lost,
Why then we racke the valew, then we find
The vertue that possession would not shew us
Whiles it was ours . . .

[IV. I. 218–22]

As John Russell Brown says,

If Benedick truly loves he must—as Claudio must—believe
his lady's "soul" against all outward testimony: he had called
her inward spirit a "fury", but, if he has truly looked upon
her with a lover's imagination he will have seen the beauty
of that spirit and will now trust and obey.[4]

The Claudio/Hero plot, though tasteless by comparison with
that involving Beatrice and Benedick, is a variation on the same
theme. Claudio is Benedick without the advantage of seeming
capable of intellectual maturity or emotional resilience. He is, to a
large extent, a spoilt whipper-snapper, a boy thrown into the
army having acquired only the trappings of manhood and
apparently without any inward maturity. To some extent he is
more sinned against than sinning. He is the victim of his own
youthfulness, his own profession and his own class—which has
taught him little but that (like a child) he should have what he
desires. He has been provided with no inner resources by which he
can test the veracity of Don John's outrageous accusations. Like
the young hero of courtly romance, whence he comes, he responds
to every situation without thought as it comes along; his responses,
always, are self-indulgent. Equally, Hero is a conventional heroine
from courtly romance, seemingly designed to be a victim, blown
by every conventional whim dictated by the code of a literary
form which was the staple diet of the very class to which both she
and Claudio belong. She exists, as it were, only in the pages of a
book. Foakes underlines the "artificiality" of the Claudio/Hero
story.

He is a romantic lover for whom ardour is unnecessary, since
he loves an image rather than a person, and is never seen

making love to Hero. Her name signified devotion in
love, as the legendary Hero, a priestess of Venus, loved
Leander . . .[5]

The outcome of their story is "happy", as is Beatrice and Benedick's, and supposedly Claudio has learnt, as has Benedick, a
maturer conception of the nature of true love. But there is an essential difference in the effects of the two plots upon the audience's
imaginations. The Claudio/Hero story remains within convention.
Its resolution is the inevitable and mechanical result of the working-out of the ploys of a convention. The Beatrice/Benedick
resolution is based upon the logistics of the human heart and mind.
Their love, simply, is more "real" to us than that of the other two.
They have discovered one another, but Claudio and Hero have
been "put together". As Foakes says,

> These superficially romantic lovers live in a world of
> appearances and proprieties which are more important than
> personal relationships; Benedick and Beatrice are the true
> romantics, concealing their passion under a cool flow of wit.[6]

All the other characters in the play, of whatever kind—the
well-meaning Leonato and Don Pedro, the villainous Don John
and his crew, the farcically pompous Dogberry—minister to the
working-out of the two main plots. This is almost the only reason
for their existence. They are all under-developed as characters,
although two of them, Don John and Dogberry, deserve more
than a cursory mention. Don John, like the Duke in *As You Like
It*, is a man of ungovernable anger, malice, and envy. In both
cases the source of their villainy lies in their relationship to their
own brother. Don John says of his brother, "I had rather be a
canker in a hedge than a rose in his garden." He is also rancour-
ously envious of Claudio's youth, "That young start-up." O. J.
Campbell[7] reminds us that in Bandello's *novella* he is a rejected
suitor, and a bastard, and he quotes Bacon that those most subject
to envy were "deformed persons, old men and bastards".

Shakespeare does not mention rejected suitorship; he makes
little of bastardy; he concentrates on the fact of envy. There would

have been no need for him to be explicit. Such characters for the Elizabethans (the intelligentsia at least) were well-known figures of conventional literature.

It is strange how possible it is to write of so many of the ingredients of this play without feeling forced to comment on their "comic" qualities. There is much that is not comic; towards the end the play does, indeed, seem to lurch in the direction of blood and tragedy. The opening scene, Beatrice and Benedick's witty games, the garden scenes, sprinkle rather than suffuse the main theme and plot with the drops of the comic spirit. For uninhibited laughter we go decidedly and only to Dogberry.

The truth is that, in our imaginations, we are transported from one place to another by the existence of Dogberry. We move from Sicily to Warwickshire. This is, for English audiences, not only reassuring in itself but it is the means by which we are reassured that the events in Sicily will have a happy conclusion. Dogberry has all the comforting presence of the now fast disappearing village police sergeant. The very fact that he is there, largely present in the village, is sufficient. On some dark night in the Cotswolds, when evil is abroad, the great, slow-moving bulk of officialdom, galumphing against the moonlight like a large family-dog, banishes all fears that evil will triumph. The creation of Dogberry's character is far more subtle than often appears on a first acquaintance with him. He is inefficient, he is conceited, he is pompous, he is a sycophant to higher officialdom. He is all those things which we dislike when we imagine (as we often do) that they are present in the lower reaches of the civil service. Yet Dogberry is entirely lovable, and he is so largely because he gives off a sense of comfortable permanence. He stands, in his comic way, for a tested *status quo*—a symbolism which sorts well with the indigenous conservatism of the British. He is lovable, too, because he is, in a way, an implied mockery of the *status quo*—mispronouncing and malaproping his way through every situation. He is undoubtedly the mould out of which have come countless self-mocking policemen in countless comic-thriller plays. He is lovable because he is essentially warm-hearted—he has more of a care for possible broken pates in his Watch than he has for the exact execution of

B

duty. He wants all manner of things to be well, and if he seems to want to be recognised as being the creator of a happy common-wealth, we can forgive him, for it is a laudable aim. And, finally, he is lovable because, out of his own mouth, he is given words to mock his own pomposity. Like a fat copper relentlessly pursuing the wrong clue he is determined that he shall not be set down an ass. In passing judgement on himself he asserts his place in our affections. His is the triumph of naïve candour.

The language of the play, for the most part, is prose. It is per-haps partly for this reason that it lacks a full romantic glow; we have to make more of an intellectual response in order to realise that Shakespeare's theme is still basically that which he had begun to develop in the highly-wrought verse-plays of his younger days. In *Love's Labour's Lost* and *The Comedy of Errors*, particularly, he is more explicit about what he means by true and real love, and the warmly lyrical passages of verse in those plays convey the meaning with passion. In this play the basic theme has to be worked out in the rational part of the audience's experience. From the time he wrote *Henry IV* he had begun more and more to exploit prose as a dominant medium of communication. We shall never know why this happened, but we may guess at two reasons. First, Shake-speare's genius, throughout his life, was of that kind which can be described as restless in the matter of form. He was the kind of artist who obsessively needs to master whatever form, com-munication, dramatic mode urges itself upon his imagination. The prose language of *Much Ado* represents a complete mastery of the prose medium. Shakespeare shows himself capable, at differ-ent points in the play, of rendering glittering wit, malaprop farce, true tenderness, and controlled pathos—all in the medium of prose.

Second, we may guess that, at this point of fame, recognition, and relative affluence in his career, he "relaxed" his imagination (if only for a very short time) from the pressures and demands of writing dramatic poetry. This is not to say that he found the writing of prose easier than the writing of poetry, but that, after the tremendous poetic achievements of *Romeo and Juliet*, *A Mid-summer Night's Dream*, and of *Henry IV*, his imagination required, in a way, to be refreshed. The prose of *Much Ado*, in all its manifestations, seems easy-running. It may not, indeed, have come easy, but Shakespeare as an artist found refreshment not by absenting himself from creative activity, but by changing the direction and the means of his creative imagination.

When he wrote this play he was, we suspect, in a happy time. The play's dark corners are, in the end, completely suffused with the sunlight of affirming love and joyous verbal encounter. Yet, the period of relaxation was short. The subsequent plays—*As You Like It* and *Twelfth Night*—show how much, poetically, he had benefited from this exquisite excursion into prose.

As You Like It

In his introduction to a volume of translations of Elizabethan love stories used by Shakespeare as the source for some of his plays, T. J. B Spencer writes:

> [Shakespeare] had the ability to go and find out the best that was known and thought in his day; to get it quickly (as a busy writer must, for Shakespeare wrote a million words in twenty years); to get it without much trouble and without constant access to good collections of books . . . to deal with his materials and sources of information with intelligence and discrimination. . . . Perhaps he was a good listener, not self-assertive in the company of his supposed "betters", and was therefore able, with that incomparable celerity of mind of his, to profit from any well-informed acquaintance.[8]

As You Like It is an excellent demonstration of Spencer's remarks. The play was written in 1599, at a time when the vogue for pastoral romance was at its height and when the taste for it was satisfied by plays like Munday's *The Downfall of Robert, Earl of Huntington*[9] and *The Death of Robert, Earl of Huntington*, by Munday and Chettle,[10] and by popular translations from Italian *novelle*. Shakespeare had the ability to find the best and, indeed, the most popular. His source for this play was Thomas Lodge's *Rosalynde, Euphues' Golden Legacie*.[11] He "received" his source quickly enough to catch the height of fashion. His intelligence and dramatic skill are triumphantly proved in the extent to which the original source is deepened in meaning, enlivened in incident, sharpened in characterisation. His own penetrating imagination transformed Rosalynde from a typical pastoral-romantic heroine into one of the most pleasingly devious and full-blooded young women in theatre history. That same imagination gave the romantic material of the play a piquant sauce by its invention of Touchstone, Audrey, William, and Oliver Martext, and a disturbing source for speculation in the creation of Jaques. As to what he was able to acquire and utilise by being a good listener— picking up unconsidered trifles and transforming them into gold— this play, again, gives ample testimony. In the characters of Touchstone and Jaques there may be seen the outcome of the impact made by the entry of Robert Armin[12] into the company. Armin replaced the "natural" clown Will Kempe, and his arrival is signalled by the appearance in Shakespeare's plays of a new kind of character, built from basically comic material but presenting a face to the world of the play, and to the audience, which gives indications of something beyond mere comic communication and response.

What Shakespeare has done with his source has the eventual result of making much more complex the meaning behind the fable and, certainly, of raising the play beyond the rut of typical pastoral comedy. The stark contrasts between sunshine and shadow, the conventional behaviour, the typed characters, the mechanical resolution of the plot—all of which are typical of pastoral romance—are present in *As You Like It* but they are held within a form whose boundaries, shape, and texture are elastic and of rich material. The play is, so far, the maturest exploration of a vision of love and its meaning. Despite the quality of the fable and the action, despite the fact that this forest of Arden has about it something of the never-never aspect of contrived romance, the exploration of the theme is sharply realistic. The audience is able to enjoy the play on two levels. It is allowed to gambol its imaginations in the delights of the fable, but it would be an insensitive theatregoer who did not realise that the theme reaches deeply into the meaning of love and the irony of life.

In general terms Shakespeare develops the theme already announced in the early comedies—the necessity of order, fidelity,
truth, and honour for a successful outcome in love. We have seen
the working-out of the theme of order (and its opposite) in the
history plays; in this play, for the first time with mature tenderness and emotional warmth, the working-out of the theme is seen
not through historical process but in the geography of the human
heart.

Rosalind is at the centre of the action and the theme—she is both
the "creator" of right order, and its most positive and acceptable
symbol. Her "teaching" to Orlando of the ways of love is a
demonstration of the theme in depth, her conducting and dispos-
ing of the love-affairs of others is a demonstration of the theme
latitudinally. Her education of Orlando is never sententious; the
need for love to be certain and faithful is never preached at him.
She teaches by the example of her own feelings, and her serious-
ness of purpose is expressed in quick flashes, quick-silver proofs
that, for her, all the gamesomeness and the antics in the forest, are
more than words and appearances.

> Good my complection, dost thou think though I am
> caparison'd like a man, I have a doublet and hose in my
> disposition?
>
> [III. II. 181–3]

The absence of sententiousness allows Rosalind to stand as an
example of the best kind of woman—gay, tender, loyal, witty,
faithful, and spritely in body and mind. The love she teaches she
also embodies. The keynote of her character is a delicacy of spirit.
There is no other character in the play whose reactions we can
trust, respect, and delight in, with the same confidence she inspires
in us.

Shakespeare exploits this delicacy of spirit in a number of ways.
Her recoiling from physical injury,

> But is there any else longs to see this broken Musicke in his
> sides? Is there yet another doates upon rib-breaking?
>
> [I. II. 125–7]

Her generosity,

> The little strength that I have, I would it were with you.
> [I. II. 174-5]

Her courageous sincerity,

> Unlesse you could teach me to forget a banished father, you
> must not, learne mee how to remember any extraordinary
> pleasure.
> [I. II. 2-5]

She emerges as the leader of the trio which, self-banished from
court, ventures into the forest of Arden. In taking up the leadership, she loses nothing of her femininity, and this is constantly re-
affirmed by Shakespeare in those fleeting glimpses we have of her
vulnerability to love.

> What did he when thou saw'st him? What sayde he?
> How look'd he? Wherein went he? What makes hee heere?
> Did he aske for me?
> [III. II. 205-8]

The audience is thus prepared to accept, without embarrassment,
her obvious mental superiority to Orlando, and her determination
to take the reins into her own hands. All the lineaments of her
character are enchanting to our eyes and ears, but her true position
in the play amounts to more than enchantment. There is another
quality in her which is likely to be obscured by her more dominant
qualities. Rosalind has within her a secret sadness, which often
takes the form of a reflective wryness; this never becomes bitter
but gradually comes to be seen as the real source of her honesty
and of her insistent quest for plain-dealing in love.

The first appearance of this element in her character comes in
Act One, scene two, in an exchange with Celia which is inter-
rupted by Touchstone. His intervention side-tracks the conversa-
tion into witty badinage, but we have heard enough before his
entrance to make us reflect upon Rosalind's words:

> Fortune reigns in gifts of the world, not in the lineaments of
> Nature.
> [I. II. 38-9]

Fortune has dealt hard with her and, quite soon, it is to deal her another, harder blow, by the Duke's decree of banishment. She has been prevented by Fortune from enjoying the full happiness which her own personality, her social status and the companion-ship of close relatives would have given her. She knows from her own experience the truth of her own remark about Fortune and she alludes to its meaning again when, after Orlando has defeated the wrestler, she hopefully declares,

> He cals us back: my pride fell with my fortunes.
> [I. II. 231]

She has been the victim of bad fortune; she has learned that it is realistic not to expect too much from "Nature". Man is a creature dominated by the unprophecible operations of good or bad fortune. She can scarcely credit the possibility that love has entered her heart; what kind of fortune is it, now, that has put Orlando's image into her mind?—this is the unspoken question. The question remains unspoken throughout the play, but the assiduousness with which Rosalind tries to discover whether a true and good nature lies behind the fortune that has brought Orlando to her, suggests that the question is never far from being uttered. She is equally assiduous in ensuring that Phoebe and Corin will behave in accordance with nature. What nature is, is double-edged; it may be ugly or beautiful, fickle or faithful—it is important that its true lineaments should be discovered.

> But Mistris, know your selfe, downe on your knees
> And thanke heaven, fasting, for a good mans love;
> For I must tell you friendly in your eare,
> Sell when you can, you are not for all markets.
> [III. V. 57–60]

The forest of Arden—the palpable form of nature—is where better selves are found. The rancour and fury of Duke Frederick is converted into a happy piety; the jealousy and distrust of Orlando's brother is transmuted into warm affection. The banished Duke and his men have already discovered a relaxed companionable ease when we meet them; they have learnt mutual respect and inter-dependence—an ordered society.

In marked contrast to the natural life is the court. There, sharp anger erupts suddenly; violence is near the surface in the confrontation between Orlando and Charles, and in the motives behind it; inhuman cruelty is implicit in the burning of Orlando's house. There is a touching symbolism in the fact that the most "naturally good" man in the court—old Adam—feels that he must leave. When he is received graciously and kindly by the banished Duke's society, it is as if he has returned to his source. He comes, we feel, to die happily in his right and proper soil.

Only two people remain untouched by the translation from the sophisticated artificial court where capricious fortune operates, to the forest where beneficent nature works—Touchstone and Jaques.

Touchstone is no mere allowed fool, and not a natural idiot. He is a man of sophistication who has become part of the organisation of the court. His confrontation with Corin confirms this and, at the same time, illustrates clearly the kind of contrast which the whole play communicates—that between the simple efficacy of what is beneficently natural as opposed to the deviousness of what is sophisticated. Touchstone is worsted by Corin, whose natural common sense overcomes the verbal dexterity of self-conscious wit.

> Not a whit *Touchstone*, those that are good manners at the Court, are as ridiculous in the Countrey, as the behaviour of the Countrie is most mockeable at the Court. You told me, you salute not at the Court, but you kisse your hands; that courtesie would be uncleanlie if Courtiers were shepheards.
>
> [III. II. 41–5]

His wooing of the conspicuously "natural" Audrey is little more than a kind of charade. His tone to her is always mocking. "Doth my simple feature content you?" he asks her, and this leads him to a display of word-mongering in the middle of which something of his sardonic philosophy of life is revealed.

Amen. A man may if he were of a fearful heart, stagger in
this attempt: for heere wee have no Temple but the wood,
no assembly but horne-beasts. But what though? Courage.
As hornes are odious, they are necessarie.

[III. III. 42–7]

Touchstone performs a triple role in the play. The first is his professional one as court fool—a witty and licensed *obbligato* to the
action of the play. The second involves his thematic function (with
Jaques) as a resistant to the beneficial effects of the natural order of
the forest of Arden. What the Duke says,

> Are not these woods
> More free from perill then the envious Court?
> Heere feele we not the penaltie of *Adam*,
> The seasons difference, as the Icie phange
> And churlish chiding of the winters winde,
>
> .   .   .   .   .   .
>
> Sweet are the uses of adversitie
> Which like the toad, ougly and venemous,
> Weares yet a precious Jewell in his head:

[II. I. 3–14]

has its thematic answer in Touchstone's words to William.

> Truely Shepheard, in respect of it selfe, it is a good life; but
> in respect that it is a shepheards life, it is naught.

[III. II. 13–15]

Touchstone's third function is as a sharp sauce to contrast with the
romantic diet of the play. Shakespeare, by this time, had learnt a
lesson unapprehended in the early comedies. It was that the art of
dramatic writing is, to a large extent, that of representing contrasts
in mood, style, and character. Without the presence of Touchstone's sardonic sharpness, the romantic food would cloy and
grow tiresome.

Jaques shares this function with him; indeed, our appetites
begin to yearn for the romantic diet after the merest taste of
Jaques's sour melancholy. Yet he is much more than this. We learn

much about him before he actually appears, and it is well to take heed of the information we are given—Shakespeare is always conspicuously careful about the preliminary information which he gives his audience. What we are usually given is intended to implant in our minds a dominant characteristic (courage and martial prowess in Macbeth, melancholy grief in Hamlet, pride, status, and bravery in Othello) upon which the subsequent situations and themes of the play will work—in other words, the material which is to be tested and manipulated by circumstance.

We learn, of Jaques, that he has been observed "weeping and commenting" upon a deer that he has seen wounded by a hunter. A herd of deer sweeps past the stricken animal, and Jaques compares their hurried indifference to the ways of the human world.

> Sweepe on you fat and greazie Citizens,
> 'Tis just the fashion; wherefore doe you looke
> Upon that poore and broken bankrupt there?
> [II. I. 56–7]

We have learnt, then, of a man who, charitably, could be described as sensitive and philosophical, but might well occasion the cynical view that he is sententious and emotionally self-indulgent. We incline to the second view, when we hear the Duke say,

> I love to cope him in these sullen fits,
> For then he's full of matter.
> [II. I. 67–8]

This inclination is given some justification when we first meet Jaques. He doth protest too much about his state of melancholy; he is an inward-looking man.

> I can sucke melancholly out of a song, as a Weazel suckes egges.
> [II. V. 12–13]

There follow the superb speeches to the Duke and his followers in which he anatomises the condition of being a fool. In meeting Touchstone he has come across one he believes to be a fellow-traveller—one who finds the world an odd place but who, unlike himself, has a liberty, a charter, to blow on whom he pleases. Jaques, in these speeches, communicates an aspiration for a status which will allow him to reflect and comment upon the world without commitment to that world. He wants to be confirmed as one who uses his folly like a stalking horse and "under the presentation of that he shoots his wit".

Yet the "wit" he yearns to be able to expend is of a kind which, for him, must have a positive purpose. Tired of the world, possessed of "a melancholy of mine owne" which is the result, he tells Rosalind, of his experience of the world, he wishes to speak his mind to some purpose and so

> through and through
> Cleanse the foule bodie of th'infected world.
> [II. VII. 59–60]

We have enough evidence of Jaques, by now, to know that he could not wear the coat of wise motley properly. He lacks the ingredients of the true professional fool possessed by Touchstone— the gay, whimsical spirit which animates the truly wise fool. And yet Jaques seems sincere in his protestations to achieve a status from which he can cleanse the infected world. It remains to inquire why such a man should be found in the forest of Arden.

Many interpretations have been given of the source and nature of his character. A frequently expressed theory is that he is an extreme delineation of the Italianate Englishman who has travelled widely, become bored with experience and whose melancholy, which began as affectation, has now become an amalgam of conceit and real action-sapping sadness. Some have seen him as a lampoon on Sir John Harington, the translator of Ariosto; others as Shakespeare's comment on Jonson or Marston. The speeches given to Jaques seem, however, conspicuously free from references which could unequivocally associate him with actual people.

It is my contention that the character of Jaques came about partly as the result of Shakespeare's association with Armin, who joined the company in 1599. In his play *Foole upon Foole*, and his book *A Nest of Ninnies*,[13] Armin displayed a remarkable knowledge of fools, clowns and those shadowy entertainers—tumblers, jugglers, and so on—who earned a tenuous existence by entertaining at fairs, festivals and sometimes, by invitation, at feasts and celebrations in noble houses. In his book Armin distinguishes between natural fools who are prone to self-conceit and artificial fools who are professional in the exercise of their wit.

Jaques is a self-conceited man who has not the equipment to be the true professional, like Touchstone. He becomes, therefore, a wild card in the pack; he becomes a shadow in the sunlight of Arden. He is governed by a self-conceit which he cannot control. He aspires to do so, but is incapable of achieving it. Very soon, Shakespeare was to create another such—Malvolio—whose shadow casts, if only fleetingly, a darkness across Illyria. Later still, he was to create Thersites—a monstrous suppurating sore of a man; one in whom self-conceit has turned into the sourest rancour. Such characters, to be distinguished quite clearly from the professional "artificial" fools like Touchstone, Feste and, later, Lear's nameless Fool, have an ascending order of significance in the thematic texture of the plays they inhabit. Malvolio's presence is less tolerable than Jaques's, Thersites's presence almost completely intolerable; yet each one, as he appears, affects more and more our focus on the play. To a degree, such men are frustrated wise men, frustrated in status, frustrated in acceptance by their society. They do not have the blessing which the true fools have of "allowed" witty effrontery, of "licensed" opportunity to speak what, behind their wit, they know to be the truth. Above all, because they do not have the professional skill of entertaining, and, behind the mask of entertaining, of remaining uncommitted to that which they comment on, they lack objectivity.

Why, then, do Jaques, Malvolio, and their like, exist in the plays? Their presence can be superficially explained by regarding them as contrast-agents in a romantic world. To this extent they are a simple but effective means of subtilising the comic mode. A more searching yet more contentious explanation is that they are the palpable indications of a shift of balance in Shakespeare's view of the world. It cannot be too often emphasised that this view was all of a piece but that, from time to time, one facet is explored more searchingly than others. In the midst of the joyous and affirming romantic comedies, the darker hues of tragedy can be glimpsed. The comedies demonstrate the construction of an ordered world; the tragedies witness the destruction of order. Jaques and Malvolio are warning signs of Shakespeare's recognition that there is a kind of human belief, attitude, and action which sits ill with order and the acceptance of it. The better part of the self-indulgent Jaques sees a foul infection in the world and seeks to cleanse it—but he is defeated by his own conceit. The worst part of him nags at our enjoyment of the order which, by the ministrations of Rosalind, the play is making for. It is Jaques' presence which makes the ordered world created in Arden the more poignant and, in a sense, the more to be wondered about. The effective theatrical result is that the world of *As You Like It* seems fragile; its affirmation of the efficacy of good nature seems trapped in a present-tense. Its declaration of future intent seems an illusion.

> Play Musicke, and you Brides and Bride-groomes all,
> With measure heap'd in joy, to 'th Measures fall.
> [v. iv. 172–3]

Not least because, after that brave manifesto of happiness, the Duke and Jaques exchange these words.

> *Du. se.* Stay, *Jaques*, stay.
> *Jaq.* To see no pastime, I:what you would have,
>   Ile stay to know, at your abandon'd cave.
> [v. iv. 188–90]

Yet, while we are given leave by the play itself to speculate upon these graver issues, and while the affirming joy of the resolution seems fragile, we cannot forget how superbly happy we are made by the world Shakespeare orders for us. The comedy of the play is not only rich in quality, but of great variety. Rosalind's wit is not only sharp but warm—our laughter has, as it were, a contented smile upon its face simply because the wit has a happy purpose.

> Ile have no Father, if you be not he:
> Ile have no Husband, if you be not he:
> Nor ne're wed woman, if you be not shee.
> [v. iv. 116–18]

Touchstone's sharper arrows give us the kind of appreciative laughter we always reserve for the professional who is superbly good at his job. At times we respect him, with a little reserve, because he has the unnerving and disquieting ability to seem more clever than anyone else around him. At other times this kind of laughter loses its reserve; the wheel turns, and we find ourselves laughing at Touchstone, because the natural wise wit of the countryman confounds him. The comedy of Martext and of Audrey induces in us laughter of the most primitive kind. It is laughter which comes from a delighted feeling of complete superiority to the characters who make it. Audrey's enormous ignorance and innocent bawdy, Martext's crazy assumption of clerical status— these become the victims of our laughter, but we do not despise them because, firstly, they are themselves happy people and, secondly, they are natural people; both of them have an innocence which excuses their palpable defects.

All these forms of comic presentation and response are, however, contained within an essence whose effect suffuses them all. It is expressed by Helen Gardner:

> *As You Like It* is the most refined and exquisite of the comedies, the one which is most consistently played over by a delighted intelligence. It is Shakespeare's most Mozartian comedy. The essence is one in which intelligence and emotional sensitivity combine. In their combination we are neither over-provoked by too assiduous an exploration of intellectual meaning nor too lavish a presentation of emotional experience. It is as if Shakespeare had himself achieved a kind of civilised contentment—fleeting but true— and shared it without either exaggerating or cheapening it.[14]

Twelfth Night

Twelfth Night is Shakespeare's most emotionally pleasing romantic comedy. The glow of happiness grows stronger and stronger as the play proceeds to its conclusion; although the presence of Malvolio throws some shadow across the sunlight, it is not enough to rob the play of its prevailing climate of warmth and achieved joy.

The occasion of its first performance may well have dictated its colouring and temperature. It is a festival of love, written for a festive occasion. John Manningham[15] reports in his diary that he saw the play acted in the Middle Temple on 2 Feb. 1602, and he describes it in these words:

> At our feast wee had a play called "Twelve Night, or What You Will", much like the Commedy of Errores, or Menechmi in Plautus, but most like and neere to that in Italian called Inganni. A good practise in it to make the Steward believe his Lady Widdowe was in love with him, by counterfeyting a letter as from his Lady in generall termes, telling him what shee liked best in him, and prescribing his gesture in smiling, his apparaile, &c., and then when he came to practise making him believe they tooke him to be mad.

Leslie Hotson believes that its first performance was at court on the feast of the Epiphany in January 1601, at celebrations to honour the visit of a Tuscan ambassador—Duke Orsino.[16] Either of these occasions suggests a special commissioning of Shakespeare. The alternative title "Or What You Will" indicates a happy flippancy—the nomenclature does not matter, the occasion is the thing. Chronologically, the play seems to follow hard on the heels of As You Like It. It could not, from internal evidence, have been written before 1599 and, with Manningham's diary in mind, it could not have been written after 1602.

Shakespeare, still accepting the pressures of theatrical fashion, had been reading versions of Italian plays and novelle. There are plot-similarities with the translation of Gl'Ingannati[17] which was performed in Cambridge on the occasion of a visit by the Earl of Essex. The more direct source, however, is Barnabe Riche's story of Apollonius and Silla,[18] itself deriving ultimately from Gl'Ingannati by way of prose-versions in Bandello's Novelle, and Belleforest's Histoires Tragiques.[19]

Barnabe Riche's version contains two questions which Shakespeare's play, in some measure, answers. It asks, first, "What is the ground, indeed, of reasonable love, whereby the knot is knit of true and perfect friendship?" And then,

> To love them that hate us, to follow them that fly from us, to fawn on them that frown on us, to curry favour with them that disabuse us, to be glad to please them that care not how they offend us, who will not confess this to be an erroneous love, neither grounded upon wit nor reason?[20]

Shakespeare's answer, in effect, is to demonstrate different kinds of love—fawning love, misplaced love, witless love, unexpected love, and true love. Malvolio, Orsino and Olivia, Andrew, Sebastian, and Viola, are, in their way, agents for each particular demonstration. It might be said that Toby and Maria also play a part in this particular dance; their love is based on admiration, affection, and expediency.

Each kind of love is presented to us, and we have to make up our minds about which, in Riche's word, is the least "erroneous". The important point, however, is that whatever decision we make, we are left in no doubt that all kinds of love must play a part in the everlasting human dance.

Two kinds are announced at the very beginning of the play. Orsino's first speech has all the languid self-indulgence of a man of wealth and ease for whom love is a bitter-sweet *adagio* accompaniment to his opulent life. His personality is firmly established from the first. He is a curiously inert man, prepared only to give commands for actions to be taken by others on his behalf. He is the sort of man who is likely to live in an illusion of love, since he seems never to take steps to discover for himself the truth (or otherwise) of his languid affections.

Viola's personality is immediately established in sharp contrast. Her very manner of speaking—quick, urgent, directly questioning —seems like a fresh breeze by comparison with Orsino's hot-house phraseology. Moreover, what she says about Orsino to the sea-captain tells us of an active, purposeful creature prepared to seek the truth of emotions which stir in her. It is well to emphasise the strong possibility that she already harbours some love for Orsino from her first entrance.

I have heard my father name him.
He was a Batchellor then.

[I. II. 28–9]

O that I serv'd that Lady,
And might not be delivered to the world
Till I had made mine owne occasion mellow
What my estate is.

[I. II. 41–4]

Ile do my best
To woe your Lady: yet a barrefull strife,
Who ere I woe, my selfe would be his wife.

[I. IV. 39–41]

These are strong hints. They are, admittedly, less definite than the
source story where Viola (Silla) has previously met Orsino
(Apollonius) in her father's house where "she fed him with such
amorous baits as the modesty of a maid could reasonably afford",
but they are important enough.

Viola's personality is shown, too, in sharp contrast to Olivia's.
When she first visits the "Marble-brested" and mourning creature, we note the difference between a self-indulgent and, for the
moment, inert person and one for whom word and deed are as
one. Yet, Olivia responds to Viola's urgent sincerity and directness; we feel that her request to Viola to return again is the most
positive decision she has made in her life. Shakespeare points the
difference between the Orsino/Olivia type and Viola in this
scene, through the language. When Viola is reporting or quoting
Orsino, her language is cast in the conventional romantic mode
and phraseology.

Most radiant, exquisite, and unmatchable beautie.

[I. V. 160]

In reply to Olivia's question, "How does he love me?", she says,

With adorations, fertill teares,
With groanes that thunder love, with sighes of fire.

[I. V. 239–40]

and we are inclined to declare, "Yes, and with precious little else!" On the other hand, when Viola is speaking from her own heart and mind, the language is more direct, untainted with wild filigree.

> Make me a willow Cabine at your gate,
> And call upon my soule within the house,
> Write loyall Cantons of contemned love,
> And sing them lowd even in the dead of night.
>
> [I. V. 252–5]

In this speech she, too, is talking about the outward appearances of love, the visual and aural proofs of it, but, unlike Orsino, she gives a sense of conviction—the appearance is an earnest of a deeper validity, not an empty substitute for truth.

Viola, like Rosalind, is at the centre of the play's positive meaning. She shares Rosalind's courage, determination, fidelity and wit, but the total effect of her personality on us is quite different. There are two reasons for this. The first is that whereas Rosalind shares her disguise with both Touchstone and Celia (both talkative characters) Viola shares hers only with a sea-captain, who promises to stay mute and, indeed, disappears for much of the action. Viola, then, is virtually alone in her disguise.

The second is that Rosalind dispenses her exquisite advice on love with an extrovert largesse. Viola does not. Rosalind's position in her play is, therefore, far more public, but Viola's is private and, at times, secretive. Celia knows Rosalind loves Orlando; no one knows that Viola loves anyone. Rosalind may be vulnerable in a general sense, simply because she is a woman; Viola is vulnerable in a particular sense because she is a woman with a secret.

This gives her a quality of poignant solitariness which is not apparent in Rosalind; it is this solitariness inside her embattled emotions which makes Viola a more sweetly sad heroine than Rosalind. The latter, we feel, would be capable of enduring even more in order to achieve her love for Orlando; Viola, we suspect, has gone as far as the female can go—alone. "My Father had a daughter lov'd a man," she says, but cannot, in her secret solitariness, convey the pith of the meaning to anyone. Rosalind, on the contrary, is free, with Celia, to question and debate upon her love for Orlando. If the story of Rosalind is the pursuit of a true order of love, that of Viola is of the pursuit of the simple fact of true love.

When we see her in the midst of the love-complexes, her isolation is increased by our being able to prove from our experience of the play the truth of Orsino's remark about men.

> Our fancies are more giddie and unfirme,
> More longing, wavering, sooner lost and worne,
> Then womens are.
>
> [II. IV. 32–3]

He is indeed making a shrewd comment upon himself and, by implication, upon the other males in the play. Malvolio's "love" for Olivia is entirely self-seeking; Toby's love for Maria smacks of insurance against old age; Sebastian's love for Olivia is thrust upon him without his having to stir. Sir Andrew, perhaps, has little sense at all what love is. He is in a desperate case, seeking a contract which is impossible. He requires social status but, unconsciously, what he really needs is a show of kindness, which does not seem forthcoming.

The various kinds of love are shown with insistent clarity by Shakespeare. He does not specifically designate the relative value of each as they are displayed; rather, he gives us clear evidence, and seems to be saying—human-kind is like this. He stops short of explicit judgement, except to imply a distinction between love that is the product of fortune—ill or good—and love which is a natural growth. Malvolio's words, "'Tis but Fortune, all is fortune" may be taken as the motto of all the lovers except Viola. It underlines the contrast between the active pursuit of true love by her, and the inert or time-serving predispositions of the others.

It is, however, important to emphasise the joyous and comic direction which the play takes. To dismiss the Belch/Aguecheek/ Maria scenes as mere sub-plot is to minimise and falsify their importance in giving impetus to the play's direction. If we imagine the play without them we are left with a sense of loss and irritation. Neither Orsino nor Olivia match up, in force of personality, or integrity of purpose, to Viola. The story of these three, by itself, is a story of self-indulgence confronted by liberal humanity. The comic scenes activate the movement of the play and, importantly, create a society, a world, around what would otherwise be a claustrophobic, arras'd privacy. Illyria is not believably Illyria without Belch, Aguecheek, and Maria.

The most significant feature of the comic scenes is the clarity with which Shakespeare distinguishes the personalities. In one sense Belch and Aguecheek are in the same position. Both rely upon their "connections": in Belch's case, his family relationship with Olivia; in Aguecheek's, the tenuous associations which his (no doubt meagre) legacy might assure him. Yet, they are immensely different in temperament.

Toby Belch is a scaled-down Falstaff—one who has so far avoided being thrust out from the bosom of an outraged family, to trick and finagle his way through the darker reaches of the commonwealth. He is the black sheep of a noble family, suffered with limited patience and, perhaps, with a slight grudging acceptance of some military prowess he displayed in battles now forgotten. He has, we might conjecture, retired at some time from military service to batten upon his unsuspecting niece. It is perhaps only impecuniosity, and the necessity to ensure that sack will continue to flow, that keeps him in Illyria. He employs, now that he is stuck there, the same strategy and tactics as we imagine he employed in felling enemies and capturing booty, in his relentless picking at Aguecheek's scanty legacy. Sir Toby has reached a crisis in his life. He cannot, much longer, rely upon the continuance of Olivia's thin patience. His adventurous, reckless spirit is prepared to enter upon stratagems whose outcome he is never sure of. His participation in the gulling of Malvolio is hedged about with a queasy fear that it may do him more harm than good.

> I would we were well ridde of this knavery. If he may bee conveniently deliver'd, I would he were, for I am now so farre in offence with my Niece, that I cannot pursue with any safety this sport the uppeshot.
>
> [IV. II. 65–8]

He jests, he is one of the boys, he has "connections", but he really does not know what to do with himself. Sack, quips, cunning are almost all he has left of identity. He is like those old soldiers who, in peace-time, maunder through memory, fighting old battles, bereft by time and circumstance of any real purpose.

Yet there is a vital difference between Belch and the rootless old soldiers who, in contemporary films, plays, and pubs, are seen to be rotting because expectancy is even less certain than memory. Sir Toby Belch is not a bore. He is shifty and can be inhuman.

> *And.* Ile help you sir *Toby*, because we'll be drest together.
> *To.* Will you helpe an Asse-head, and a coxcombe, and a
>   knave: a thin fac'd knave, a gull?
>
> [v. i. 196–9]

He is sentimental and admiring when he finds a spirit as recklessly expedient as his own.

> She's a beagle true bred, and one that adores me.
> [ii. iii. 168–9]

Yet we like him because he still enjoys life and because he has the courage of his own immediate reactions to a situation. He does not attempt to fool either himself or us about his feelings. When he has eaten unwisely he is gaily honest about those "pickled herrings"; he loves his niece, in his own way, with direct admiration.

> Ile drinke to her as long as there is a passage in my throat, and drinke in Illyria.
> [i. iii. 36–8]

He makes no bones about what he is doing to Sir Andrew.

> I have beene deere to him lad, some two thousand strong, or so.
> [iii. ii. 51–2]

In fact he is an honest rogue. But, more than this, he is a rogue who can accommodate his words to the reality of a situation. He is sensitive to events and the verbal means by which those events can

be embodied. In the drunken way, his words have the slithering
largesse of bonhomie induced by alcohol.

> To heare by the nose, it is dulcet in contagion.
> But shall we make the Welkin dance indeed? Shall wee
> rowze the night-Owle in a Catch, that will drawe three
> soules out of one Weaver? Shall we do that?
>
> [II. III. 55–9]

In the cunning way of strategy, his words smack of "fashion" calculated to persuade Sir Andrew that he is at the centre of modish-
ness.

> *And.* And I thinke I have the backe-tricke, simply as strong
> as any man in Illyria.
> *To.* Wherefore are these things hid? Wherefore have these
> gifts a Curtaine before 'em? Are they like to take dust, like
> mistris *Mals* picture? Why dost thou not goe to Church in
> a Galliard, and come home in a Carranto?
>
> [I. III. 115–22]

In the gamesome way, he affects the grandeur and solemnity of
vital military deeds, pregnant with sombre implications.

> That defence thou hast, betake thee too't: of what nature
> the wrongs are thou hast done him, I knowe not; but
> thy intercepter full of despight, bloody as the Hunter,
> attends thee at the Orchard end.
>
> [III. IV. 210–14]

He may be a man for all seasons, but he is a stylist, and no man of
real style can ever be boring.

Sir Andrew is a natural victim for such a man. He was, we suspect, born into the world with the extreme liability of being the
most mentally underdeveloped son of a family of some means. He
has been sent off to find what fortune he can, with limited means
that will soon, with the depradations of Sir Toby, be frittered away.
One cylinder is not firing at all in the clattering engine of his mind.
He is always out of phase with the circumstances of the moment.
He comes around the corner, hopefully, just at that moment when

faster creatures have left. He utters modish precepts like an auto-
maton, but we can be sure that nothing of account is moving in
his brain.

> *And.* Good Mistris accost, I desire better acquaintance.
> *Ma.* My name is *Mary* sir.
> *And.* Good mistris *Mary*, accost.
> *To.* You mistake knight: Accost, is front her, boord her,
>   woe her, assayle her.
>
> [I. III. 49–53]

He is essentially a creature to be laughed *at* not *with*, but by the
same token, he is one to be sympathised with simply because he is
comically defenceless.

Not so Malvolio. He is here to be scorned, though the trend of
modern stage-production reveals, yet again, that modern sensibilities cannot be content with a figure who is laughed out of court.
Malvolio and Shylock have crept into the shawl of modern
sentimentality and conscience. Ironically, we are more prepared
to condemn the black Othello than either of these two—one who
is a stupid, arrogant, weak-minded sycophant, the other who
wants flesh.

Explanations of Malvolio's character have ranged from the
notion that he is a caricature of the Puritan to an under-docu-
mented assumption that he is a picture of a real individual—Sir
William Knollys, comptroller of the royal household from 1596 to
1602.[21] Malvolio might, if we had the proof, turn out to be partly
an amalgam of both of these. Yet his dramatic presence is not
explained entirely by accepting both or either. Malvolio is mean-
spirited, ludicrously ambitious, and humourless—as perhaps some
Puritans and Sir William were. He is, however, more. In order to
establish his dramatic function, it is necessary to rid our minds of
the restricting idea that by romantic comedy we mean only delight
lyricism, and a comfortable, uncomplicated resolution. Not one of
Shakespeare's plays which are stamped with the label "romantic"
justifies those assumptions. They achieve their theatrical potency
and maintain their interest because they are superb exercises in the
art of contrast. They achieve, in their resolutions, the final picture

of an ideal condition, but the journey towards the resolution always involves the concept of an unideal world. Every word and every activity of Malvolio's is, in effect, un-Illyrian. Everything, except him, moves in a direction which will finally release happiness, correct partnership, and generosity of spirit. Even poor, funny, Sir Andrew receives, at the end, the touch of kindness he needs.

Malvolio's meanness of spirit is completely incompatible with this. All that is left for a man whose ambitions and pretensions are absurd, and who is discovered to be absurd in himself, is to cry out for revenge. It is this final cry which has occasioned so much heart-searching in modern commentators and modern audiences. To be sorry for Malvolio is to forget that the word he uses is "revenge", and to forget, too, that he has played a large part in bringing himself to this condition. He has been "ill-used", condemned to darkness, has made himself, and been made, to look and sound like a presumptuous idiot. Yet he has asked for much of this simply by breaking the rules of Illyria, by trying to be what he is not—in love with Olivia and bigger than his station. Of course she herself, as Feste sharply reminds us, is overaffected in her mourning. Viola in disguise is also, to a degree, what she is not. Orsino's misdirected passion is a measure of his own self-delusion. Yet all of these are, so to speak, purged of their illusions—by love. Only Malvolio seems completely incapable of being purged (Aguecheek would be, but is not given the opportunity) and is unequipped to adjust to the "reality" which is uncovered in Illyria, though attempts are made to enable him to make an adjustment. To some modern sensibilities these attempts seem hard and disproportionate to his faults. Yet we must disabuse ourselves of sentimentality in the light of what is revealed by the existence of Feste, and in particular, by his relationship to Malvolio.

Feste, even more than Touchstone, is an example of the best kind of Fool described by Armin. For Armin the most interesting Fool is one who has nimble wit, an ability to entertain, and who "wears not motley in his brain". Enid Welsford[22] has shown in her study of real Fools in history that there was a remarkable gallery of such men who fitted Armin's ideal. Some of the records of the courts of England which are quoted by Miss Welsford make it clear that a number of the allowed Fools of noble and royal households were men of notable intellectual distinction. Thomas More's Fool—Henry Paterson—was an accepted member of the household, eating with the family and joining in their devotions. Henry VIII's Fool—Will Somers—was a remarkable man, vying in wit and political shrewdness with Will Patch—Wolsey's Fool. These two entertainers served two of the most powerful men in England. They were cousins who had the ears of two men destined to clash. The fancy revolves about the possibility of secrets that were heard by both of them, but fact itself gives us a glimpse of the power that they wielded.

> When they [i.e. Patch and Somers] tapped a hogshead,
> however, they found that the wine would not flow, and
> when they smashed it to discover the reason they found that
> it was full of gold. Further investigation proved that all the
> hogsheads were being used to store treasure. Will reported
> the discovery to his master, and this was the beginning of
> the Cardinal's disgrace.[24]

Most of the Fools of whose historical existence in medieval Europe we know, with something of their activities, present a common set of characteristics which bear a remarkable similarity to those of Feste and Lear's Fool in particular and, to a lesser extent, to Touchstone's.

First, they seem to have occupied an indeterminate status in noble or royal households (in this respect Henry VIII's and More's Fools were exceptions). Very often the Fool had finally arrived at a noble or royal domicile by a series of steps from humble and lowly surroundings—from village-green entertainment to court entertainment. They do not, thereby, seem to have changed their social status in any precise sense, for such was their dependence upon pleasing their lord and master that they could, at any time, have been thrust out of doors. Yet, having physically removed themselves from an originally low social status, they could no longer be said to belong there either. In fact they seem to have existed in an odd limbo. They were classless; they slipped in and

out of the social stratifications very easily, but they were committed to none of them. Feste, in particular, exemplifies this. Like
Touchstone, he has easy commerce both with high, middle and
low; more certainly than Touchstone he seems not completely to
belong to any particular group or home. He wanders from
Orsino's court to Olivia's. He is everyone's acquaintance,
but no one's friend.

Second, the Fools of history were possessed of a license to
utter things which, if they came from another's mouth, might
have been deemed discourteous, libellous, treacherous, or disloyal.
An "allowed" Fool's license was one which was bestowed upon
him because he was regarded as entertainer and because his actual
social status was so indeterminate. He had the privilege of comment only because he was uncommitted in social and human
terms. Both Touchstone and Feste exercise this license to the full.
Feste, we suspect, is the only one who would have been allowed to
say to Olivia what he does say touching her mourning.

> *Clo.* Good Madona, why mournst thou?
> *Ol.* Good foole, for my brothers death.
> *Clo.* I thinke his soule is in hell, Madona
> *Ol.* I know his soule is in heaven, foole.
> *Clo.* The more foole (Madona) to mourne your Brothers
>   soule, being in heaven. Take away the Foole, Gentlemen.
>   [I. v. 61–8]

Yet there was an irony involved here. The license was tenuous and
revokable. The Fool's freedom was an illusion. Both Feste and
Lear's Fool are threatened with the whip for what they say. The
mankind of both plays cannot stand too much of the reality, the
truth, which these men utter. "He is holden wise that reputeth
himself a fool" is the hall-mark of some of the notable Fools of
history, and of Shakespeare's Fools. In the event, such a reputation
is an ironic one. It isolates the Fool, yet makes him vulnerable.

In many ways, Feste represents the most cogent dramatic version of the great Fools of history whom Shakespeare had learnt
so much about from Armin. His virtual uncommittedness to the
action is quite obvious. As R. H. Goldsmith says:

It ought to be remembered that Feste, although he confesses to a part in the intrigue, actually is not present at the baiting of the yellow-stockinged, cross-gartered gull. Instead, his rôle as ironical commentator is taken over by the less subtle Fabian.[24]

This posture of near-isolation—as if the Fool were holding himself back in order to preserve the freedom to exercise his license—is confirmed when we examine the famous drunken scene with Aguecheek and Belch. In this scene the Fool is performing his proper function of being an entertainer. He is expected to be so, and he falls into his act with natural ease. It is remarkable, however, that as soon as Maria reveals the plot against Malvolio, Feste plays no further part in the scene. In the production at the then Memorial Theatre at Stratford in 1955, the withdrawal from action was poignantly underlined by the Fool's retreat from the drunken activities, to take up a position beneath a table where he strummed quietly and thoughtfully upon an instrument, while intrigue stirred above him.

The sense that the relationship between the Fool and others is on a commercial, rather than emotional or intellectual base, is emphasised in Act Five, scene one. Here, Feste has indulged in some witty badinage with the great Duke Orsino. For a moment he seems part of the company—then this happens.

> *Du.* Thou shalt not be the worse for me, there's gold.
> *Clo.* But that it would be double dealing sir, I would you
>   could make it another.
> *Du.* O give me ill counsell.
> *Clo.* Put your grace in your pocket sir, for this once, and
>   let your flesh and blood obey it.
>
> [v. i. 24–8]

Immediately, the truth of the Fool's position is revealed. It is allowed, tolerated, the function it performs is paid for.

Why then, does Feste seem to commit himself so much to the attempt to purge Malvolio of his "madness"? If withdrawal, a desire to hide behind the mask of folly in order to shoot forth

their wit and truth, is the real motivation of Shakespeare's Fools,
why should Feste thus expose himself and endanger his freedom of
comment? In the Sir Topas scene, Feste mercilessly taunts Malvolio before eventually declaring that he will deliver the protesting
letter to Olivia.

> Madman thou errest: I say there is no darknesse but
> ignorance, in which thou art more puzel'd then the
> Aegyptians in their fogge.
>   [IV. II. 41–3]

It is this scene which, above all, renders the modern conscience
uneasy about what is being done to Malvolio.

The occasion of Twelfth Night is the feast of the Epiphany. The
ceremonies performed on this occasion have been thoroughly
described by many historians. The element which concerns us is
the Feast of Fools, performed widely in Western Europe, including
England, during the Middle Ages. Churches and cathedrals were
taken over by the irreverent—Fools, clowns, tumblers, riff-raff of
society—and a ceremony guying the rites and customs of religion
was indulged in, involving obscenity and profanity. At these
events, the chief figure—the Lord of Misrule—presided over the
noisy and chaotic activities. He did so in the guise of priest or
bishop, shouting dog-Latin, guying the litany, substituting low
comic business for church ritual. The tradition of a connection
(however bizarre) between cleric and Fool (who, the records show,
was often cast as Lord of Misrule) is both long and tenuous. It may,
for example, be implied by the extraordinary number of depictions
of Fools found carved under misericord seats in English churches
(notably at Beverley in Yorkshire, and at Worcester Cathedral).
These figures constitute the largest individual type to be found in
these church carvings. Welsford records that an Arabian jester, Si
Djoha, "was sometimes represented as a learned man with pupils,
who is consulted on matters of physical health, and has some reputation for sanctity".[25] The tradition of the clerical Fool is persistent
in both Near-Eastern and Western history.

> During the first centuries of the Christian era . . . the old
> pagan rites not only survived . . . they actually penetrated

into the interior of the churches and at length gave rise to
that famous clerical saturnalia in which mighty persons were
humbled, sacred things profaned, laws relaxed and ethical
ideals reversed, under the leadership of a Patriarch, Pope, or
Bishop of Fools.[26]

The ceremony of the Feast of Fools is known to have been performed in England (the last recorded occasion was at Beverley in
the fifteenth century) and modified versions of it were performed
on Twelfth Night at the Inns of Court. The appearance of Feste as
a cleric in *Twelfth Night* to purge a madman would, one
suspects, have been no surprise to students of the Middle Temple or
indeed to a public or private audience to whom the Twelfth Night
ceremonies were an accepted part of the actual experience of their
folk memory.

Feste, in this scene, is therefore not stepping out of his posture as
relatively uncommitted observer of the human scene. We must
not take the scene too literally. Feste, as Sir Topas, is fulfilling the
function of clerical Fool—guying, mocking, and purging, or at
least going through the motions of purging. As he puts on the
gown of Sir Topas he says, "I would I were the first that ever dis-
sembled in such a gowne." This is a neat double-edged comment
—first on the iniquities of some priests, and a reference to the long
tradition of the Fool become cleric. The irritant of Malvolio in the
play is subjected therefore to comic purging—and it is on this level
that the Elizabethan audience would have accepted it. Malvolio is
"mad" only in the sense that his disposition is at odds with the
play's disposition. He is driven "mad" by fooling, and his medicine,
for the Elizabethans, was properly administered by a Fool. The
fact that it does him no good, does not cure him so as to accept the
prevailing climate of Illyria, is neither here nor there. Lords of
Misrule have to have their victims, and if the victim is a pompous
ass with an aversion to "cakes and ale" like Malvolio, so much
more is the comic experience.

Feste, in a comic context, fulfils that function of the Fool most
seriously adumbrated by Jaques in *As You Like It*.[27] He is to be
free, withal, to comment, he is to blow wisdom through his folly

and, given the opportunity, he will purge the folly of the infected world if it will patiently receive his message.

At the time he wrote this play Shakespeare had learnt from Armin much of the fascinating story of the nature of true Fools. In that mysterious way in which imaginative need transmutes actuality into something else, Shakespeare had begun to solve a problem. More and more his plays now began to demonstrate that there was a pressing compulsion in him to present a world, but at the same time to ensure for himself a freedom by which he could comment upon that world. He had become, one may guess, growingly dissatisfied with mere revelation of a world. All his plays, from the very beginning, hold within themselves the element of comment dissociated from the actions which he created with such apparent ease. By the time he came to write *Twelfth Night* he had achieved his success. He was catering for the romantic appetites of audiences, and perhaps he had some surface contentment in his own life. At the same time he was approaching the middle years, and that part of his spirit which had always incited him never to take or create matters at their face value came to haunt him, and demand more palpable expression. The Fool is the means of that palpable expression. The Fool was an entertainer—so was Shakespeare. The Fool, as part of his professional function created, through his wit, a world of illusion—so did Shakespeare. The Fool, as Armin had taught him, used illusion and wit, but this was a mere frontage to his lonely apprehension of the truth behind illusion—and Shakespeare as dramatist had always known the value of such a usage. We see the beginnings in Feste more certainly than we do in Touchstone of what amounts to a new order of characterisation in Shakespeare's plays. It is an order which is best and most simply described as fulfilling more than one function in the play. The Fool, and of course Lear's Fool is the ultimate embodiment of this, is, on the one hand, professional entertainer— a natural inhabitant of the world of the play. Yet he is also a non-naturalistic agent—a means by which Shakespeare is able to express, and we are enabled to receive, a dimension of imaginative truth which the play's action does not, of itself, demonstrate. The Fool is as lonely as the artist; he, like the artist, creates matter to beguile, to please, to incite, to entertain. Yet, like the artist, he holds some things very close to his chest—a knowledge, a truth, an ironic vision, a wry reflection, which in the end becomes a poignant and sharp comment on the beguiling illusions the imagination has created. Feste's song at the end of the play is to be celebrated not only because the traditional tune by which (despite new versions) we remember it is so plangent and bitter-sweet, but for a more telling reason. Its sentiments embody, if naïvely, the nature of the Fool's status—aware of the eternal hard irony of reality amidst the illusion with which mankind surrounds himself. A production which gets nearest to the heart of this play is one which, at the end, leaves Feste alone on the stage, while the citizens of Illyria fade into a receiving darkness. They have, one might say, existed only in the mind and imagination of Feste, and now he dismisses them. The realist has charmed us and himself by satisfying our yearnings to be told of happy places and happy times—now it is time to turn the face away from the sunlight. Feste does so, and in his eyes we catch an expression of sadness and grief which, we suspect, comes from his own creator.

3

THE "PROBLEM" PLAYS

Troilus and Cressida, All's Well That Ends Well, and *Measure for Measure* are commonly designated "problem" plays. Scholarly definitions of this term have shown, over a long period of time, tremendous variety of emphasis. The most frequent gloss concerns the so-called "tone" of the plays, because they do not fit in either with the happy atmosphere of the romantic comedies or with the awesome darkness of the great tragedies. They are, therefore, regarded by some as problems because they are "in-between"; at one moment they seem to be taking us in the direction of comedy, at another only a tragic destination seems possible or plausible. Their apparent indeterminacy is increased by the emotional and intellectual stance which the playwright seems to have taken up in relation to the incidents and characters. He seems to look upon them with eyes which are sometimes sharply satirical or cynical, and sometimes have a grave moralising stare. He seems to want it both ways—to show humanity in its most unpleasant guise and to remind us that it also has a thoughtful, pleasing, and caring aspect. Parolles, Thersites, and Angelo leave bitter tastes in our mouths. Helena, the Duke, the Countess of Rossillion, despite the fact that some of their actions are not entirely unquestionable, allow us to taste of the better part of mankind.

So these plays may be deemed "problems" in that their ultimate meaning is difficult to grasp—in the sense that we are put in an unusual situation (where Shakespeare is concerned) of not knowing whether his habitually optimistic view of life has deserted him or not. The impression of a drive towards the demonstration and proof of the existence of order in the universe is far less certain. There is, admittedly, a theatrically-contrived resolution of the "disorder" in *All's Well* but, on a simple level, we must have pause to doubt whether, for example, the positive virtues of Helena and the fickle temperament of Bertram will ever make good bedfellows. Certainly, in *Measure for Measure*, lives are saved, unpleasant situations are, so to speak, corrected, but the means by which all this is brought about do not really allay a certain moral uneasiness which we feel. Indeed, the coming together of man and woman at the end of the play seems the result less of an inevitable ordering than of a theatrical theorem. In *Troilus and Cressida*, designated by some critics as a comedy, placed in the First Folio between the histories and the tragedies, and omitted from a recent collection of essays on Shakespeare's comedies,[1] on the grounds that it is "a tragedy or tragic satire", we are, equally, left in a puzzled frame of mind. The play talks much of the need for "order" but it demonstrates, with fierce cynicism, the opposite.

The plays, then, refuse to conform to the usual designations of comedy or tragedy; but neither are they all satire. More pertinently, they do not seem to have Shakespeare's typical sense of balance—by which the motivation of character and the actuality of situation move together harmoniously. Our critical sensibilities are split; we find ourselves involved in making moral judgements on characters on the basis of what they say, or what is said about them but, at the same time, their actions apparently contradict the judgements we have been led to make. The case of Helena is a sharp example. Her "goodness" is unquestionable, but the ease with which she allows herself to be impregnated by Bertram (for this is what it amounts to) when he believes he is taking another woman bewilders our opinion of her. It is not morally satisfying to say that, after all, Bertram is her husband and that, therefore, she is not committing a sin or a covert trick. The truth of the matter is that she diminishes herself in our estimation. She has, in a sort, tried to buy love when, all the time, we have been led to believe that she, of them all, is the one whose moral and emotional correctness and tact we can trust.

Neither is it satisfying to explain the contradictions between

C

what we are led to believe about characters and what they actually do, by falling back on the argument that we must accept these plays as, in some degree, examples of conventional plots and incidents and character-types; it is not enough to know that resolutions do occur in theatrical formulae, and that the means are devices which we must accept at their theatrical face-value. If we compare our experience of these plays with that of the romantic comedies, we are aware of a disturbing hiatus. The incidents of *As You Like It* are, equally, based on conventional plot-lines and, in their familiar sinews, there is duplicity, equivocation, and false-dealing. Yet, in the long run, a total reconciliation between structure and meaning takes place. In the problem plays Shakespeare forces us to come to certain intellectual conclusions while, at the same time, contradicting their validity. As William Empson says of *Measure for Measure*:

> In a way, indeed, I think this is a complete and successful work of the master, but the way is a very odd one, because it amounts to pretending to write a romantic comedy and in fact keeping the audience's teeth slightly but increasingly on edge.[2]

Yet, can it be that we are uneasy with these plays because we are suffering the shock of finding Shakespeare writing in a new form —one totally unexpected after what we have known from him before? From 1599 onwards Shakespeare had to contend with the shrewdly keen genius of Ben Jonson. His *Every Man Out of his Humour*, probably first produced at the new Globe Theatre in that year, introduced a new type of play which caught the interest of an audience ever ready to try out their appetites on new stuff. Jonson himself called the play "a comicall satyre". He had ransacked classical comedy and Comedia dell'Arte seeking material to satisfy his talent for ridicule, satire, and cutting comment. His characteristic method was to set up a figure, notable for folly or knavery, to draw out these qualities in an exaggerated form, and then either to show him reformed or, as in *Volpone*, to push him into the outer darkness beyond redemption.

Cases have been made for Malvolio and Parolles as Jonsonian character-types. Certainly the pretences of both are mercilessly exposed. Thersites has many of the characteristics of Jonson's misanthropes—the men who stand back and castigate folly with a display of verbal destructiveness. Mosca is typical.

> Are not you he, that filthy covetous wretch,
> With the three legges, that, here, in hope of prey,
> Have, any time this three yeare, snuft about,
> With your most grov'ling nose; and would have hir'd
> Mee, to the pois'ning of my Patron?
>
> [*Volpone*, v. III. 67–71]

Jonson's view of the world was shrewd in observation, merciless in judgement, and cynical in hue. That gentleness of spirit which is so characteristic of Shakespeare's vision of humankind, was absent in him. His knowledge of the contemporary conditions and activities of his society was, on the evidence of his plays, not only starker than Shakespeare's but excited a bigger portion of his imagination. The two men may have rejoiced in each other's company, admired each other's words, but the worlds that excited them were utterly apart.

Nevertheless, Shakespeare was an artist who rarely failed to respond to the challenge of new modes in the theatre. It was not only in his nature to do so, but expedient for his livelihood. He not only knew Jonson well but probably played in *Every Man in his Humour*. He was, undoubtedly, very aware that Jonson's drama was new, powerful, and a certain rival to his own. An explanation, then, for the sharp dissonances, the seeking out and destruction of order, the puzzling inconsistencies between character and action, the access of cynicism, in the problem plays, may be found in an attempt by Shakespeare to combat Ben Jonson by taking up this new mode of comic satire.

> The strong infusion of satire in the "problem" plays accounts to a considerable degree for their dark and pessimistic tone. If these plays give the impression that their disparate elements are imperfectly fused, it may be that Shakespeare was forcing his art into channels incongenial to his mind and art.[3]

This is a persuasive explanation which could account for much in the plays, yet it does not completely satisfy. Shakespeare, in his earlier days, had not found satire incongenial to him. *Love's Labour's Lost* is absolute testimony to this. Neither had he found the depiction of self-indulgence, duplicity, folly, inimical to him— Armado, Holofernes and others in the gallery of his satire are ample evidence. There is, perhaps, a factor missing in this explanation of why the plays are "problems".

It may be suggested that there is a further group of possibilities, none of which deny that Shakespeare was, to some extent, striving to emulate Jonson; they do, however, modify the degree and the nature of his addiction to the Jonsonian mode.

They are based on an assumption that the undoubted strains of pessimism and cynicism which so considerably mutate his essentially optimistic view of the universe, are the result of a personal catastrophe which overwhelmed him at the time of writing these plays. If this is true, it might be added that he would have been more inclined to embrace Jonson's conception of humanity. But at once we enter into the dangerous quicksands of biography. Speculation can twist and turn, while the truth keeps eluding it with ironic finality. In these three plays the hero or heroine loves another who is obviously unworthy of love. Had Shakespeare recently been unrequited? In all three plays lies and cruelty originating in a third party injure the prospects of love. Had Shakespeare been treacherously deceived in a friend? In all three plays what "seems" and what "is" are at extreme variance. Had Shakespeare undergone some deep and pessimistic self-questioning? All three plays were written near the turn of the century. Had Shakespeare fallen a victim to the *mal de siècle* which is characteristic of such times, and was notably so upon the death of Elizabeth in 1601? Sex shows its uglier side in these plays. Had Shakespeare contracted syphillis—a disease as notorious for inducing deep pessimism as for its physical unpleasantness?

All these possibilities, and others, have from time to time been put forward as explanations. Such, indeed, is the nature of the plays, that each one can be given an illusory support by the careful ordering of themes, motivations, image-clusters—but they remain illusory because they are unprovable.

Yet there may be some shadow of credibility about them. It may best be examined by noting the probable dates of the plays' composition. G. K. Hunter writes, "The two plays to which *All's Well* seems most closely related are *Hamlet* and *Measure for Measure*." Further, he notes that, "*Measure for Measure* and *All's Well* are obvious twins."[4] An area of feasible dating for the three plays is 1601 to 1604, in the order (1) *Hamlet*, (2) *All's Well*, (3) *Measure for Measure*. If we add *Troilus and Cressida* (1601–2), we are faced with a group of plays which, overall, shows marked, even severe, differences in tone and theatrical treatment from anything he had ever written before—with the possible exception of *Julius Caesar* (1599). Even more to the point, Shakespeare was, after this "problem" period, never to relinquish entirely the darker vision of existence which is found in these plays. With varying degrees of intensity and emphasis, what he communicates in his subsequent plays is evidence of a firm realisation that the mixture of good and evil, light and shade, order and disorder, is of a far more complex nature than he had hitherto comprehended. To put it crudely, a sense of the tragedy of human existence, and the inequality of motivation and action came to occupy an equal place with that characteristic optimism which, one suspects, he was born with. We do not know the external or internal reasons which caused this change in the focus of his vision. We can merely note it and marvel that what happened to his imagination as a result, far from eroding his dramatic genius, eventually shaped it to an even greater architecture.

The position, then, might be that *Hamlet* was written as the first outright manifestation of his sense of complexity; that the problem plays attempted to express it with a due regard to the modes and methods of Ben Jonson. The problem they present to us, in interpretation, can be regarded as a direct reflection of the enormous challenge Shakespeare gave himself in trying to wrestle with an unfamiliar inner force and to represent it objectively in a relatively new mode of expression. The triumph of the problem plays is that they are such forceful images of the turmoil within

Shakespeare's mind; that, theatrically, they are so effective; and
that they encompass a number of characters worthy to stand with
the best Shakespeare ever created. Their failure amounts to a lack
of correlation between their thematic ideas and the embodiment
of these in character. What Clifford Leech says of *Measure for
Measure*[5] may stand for all of them. Referring to the play's
"morality framework", its "incidental satire", its "deep probing
into the springs of action", he concludes, "Only if we concentrate
our attention on one of these aspects will the play leave us content." One might add, in agreeing with Leech, that if we do try to
concentrate on all the plays' aspects we find ourselves not only dis-
contented, but very liable to judge them as being dramatically
unsound.

All's Well That Ends Well

One significant difference between Shakespeare's source (Boccac-
cio's *Decameron*) and his play is that in the former Helena is rich
and besieged by suitors; in the latter her material possessions are
few. At one stroke Shakespeare has introduced an irritant into the
Bertram/Helena confrontation—it seems hardly apposite to call it
a love-story. It is her lowly status which first induces Bertram to
cavil, then to rebel, at the prospect of marrying her.

> I knowe her well:
> Shee had her breeding at my fathers charge:
> A poore Physitians daughter my wife? Disdaine
> Rather corrupt me ever.
>
> [II. III. 112–14]

In addition, Shakespeare seems at pains to emphasise the difference
in status. Helena is as sensitive to it as Bertram.

> The Count *Rossillion* cannot be my brother:
> I am from humble, he from honoured name:
> No note upon my Parents, his all noble,
> My Master, my deere Lord he is, and I
> His servant live, and will his vassall die.
>
> [I. III. 146–50]

This irritant lies at the heart of the play's meaning, and is one of the major reasons why both the progress of the action, and its resolution, are so curiously unsatisfying to our sense of fitness.

When we first meet Helena there is no equivocation whatsoever about the nature of her character, and her standing. She is secretly in love with Bertram and, at first, shares the secret only with us. She has something of the winsome grace of Viola—certain about love, yet baulked by circumstance from achieving the certainty in fact. Under the scathing and searching examination of Parolles, whose catechism on virginity is only a barely disguised pæan on lust and fornication, she shows a similar mettle to Viola—a witty presence of mind. Yet in the long scene with him we become aware that this heroine has a quality which marks her off from all her romantic colleagues. G. K. Hunter writes of this scene that ". . . the dialogue separates two soliloquies, one full of doubt and despair, the other inspired by determination to win; something has happened to Helena's mind in the interval between them".[6]

> 'Twere all one,
> That I should love a bright particular starre,
> And think to wed it, he is so above me
> In his bright radience and colaterall light.
> [I. I. 79–82]

This soliloquy, though it superficially reminds us of Viola's case, has an element of desperation never found in Viola. The second soliloquy, as Hunter says, is in a different key.

> The mightiest space in fortune, Nature brings
> To joine like, likes; and kisse like native things.
> Impossible be strange attempts to those
> That weigh their paines in sence, and do suppose
> What hath beene, cannot be. Who ever strove
> To shew her merit, that did misse her love?
> (The Kings disease) my project may deceive me,
> But my intents are fixt, and will not leave me.
> [I. I. 208–15]

Again, this reminds us of Viola's determination to be of service to

Orsino, to stay close to any opportunity for requiting her love, but it takes us further. What has happened between the two speeches is that Parolles has spoken shrewdly about virginity. Helena has a virginity she does not want to keep, but knows of no way to spend it to conform with her deepest desires. In a sense what is more important than actual events between these two speeches is what their difference reveals about Helena's mind. It is restless; it veers freely from one mood to another and, in so doing, it gives us opportunity to consider that there is a kind of desperation in her personality. She has determination, wit, and imagination—like Viola, and Rosalind—but we are left wondering how predictable her actions might be; there is something disturbingly imponderable about her.

When we meet her in the company of the Countess, the sense of a volatility of temperament is increased. Now she is cautious, almost mulishly taciturn, in her first replies to the Countess's questions, and in her general address.

> Mine honorable Mistris.
>
> That I am not.
>
> You are my mother Madam, would you were so that my
> Lord your sonne were not my brother.
>
> Good Madam pardon me.
>
> [I. III. 129–76]

Her veering moods and attitudes are, it becomes clear by the end of this scene, very much the result of her awareness of her social inferiority.

> O then give pittie
> To her whose state is such, that cannot choose
> But lend and give where she is sure to loose.
> [I. III. 204–6]

Never before had Shakespeare placed such an emphasis upon the effects of social status on the course of true love. Previously this had been no more than a conventional element in the easily vaulted barriers to the consummation of love. Viola "appears" to be of lowly status; her problem merely consists of biding her time until her "true" status can be revealed.

> O that I serv'd that Lady,
> And might not be delivered to the world
> Till I had made mine owne occasion mellow
> What my estate is.
>
> [*Twelfth Night*, I. II. 41–4]

Yet, on the third occasion when we meet Helena, when she visits the King to administer her medicine, a transformation seems to have taken place. This does not seem to be the Helena we have known before. She comes, certainly, as a suppliant to the King; she has come, in a way, to buy status—in order to buy love—but now she speaks with a different voice; she speaks with unsycophantic humility.

> And hearing your high Majestie is toucht
> With that malignant cause, wherein the honour
> Of my deare fathers gift, stands cheefe in power,
> I come to tender it, and my appliance,
> With all bound humblenesse.
>
> [II. I. 109–12]

She has a grave wisdom.

> Inspired Merit so by breath is bard,
> It is not so with him that all things knowes
> As 'tis with us, that square our guesse by showes:
> But most it is presumption in us, when
> The help of heaven we count the act of men.
>
> [II. I. 147–51]

She has courage.

> If I breake time, or flinch in property
> Of what I spoke, unpittied let me die,
> And well deserv'd: not helping, death's my fee,
> But if I helpe, what doe you promise me?
>
> [II. I. 186–9]

The King says of her,

> Methinks in thee some blessed spirit doth speak
> His powerfull sound within an organ weake.
>
> [II. I. 174–5]

When she is called before the court to make choice of her husband, it is as if a goddess were being presented.[7] The reactions of the various people present are deferential to the point of awe.

> *Hel.* Gentlemen, heaven hath through me, restor'd the king
>   to health.
> *All.* We understand it, and thanke heaven for you.
>
> [II. III. 63–5]

The transformed Helena has, indeed, overcome by her wisdom, goodness, and healing power, any petty considerations of inferior status. In fact, long before this, even in Act One, no one except Bertram and herself has estimated her by any measure other than the excellent qualities of her nature. She has inherited virtues from her father; the Countess accepts her as a daughter; Lafeu implies confidence in her. No one else seems to have any doubts about the "status" of her excellent personality, and she arrives at the King's court with conquering proof of the estimation of others.

It is at this point in the play that some consideration of the "symbolic" position to which she has been raised, is apposite. The play, as a short, simple, but powerful demonstration of the power of goodness, virtue, and love, might have ended at the King's court with the glamorous noble youth, Bertram, superior in social status, willingly accepting the hand of one to whom social status has become an irrelevancy—so certain and powerful has been the emergence of Helena's virtuous soul. Parolles, with his rabid sexuality, would have vanished from the play, vanquished by Helena's purity of spirit. G. Wilson Knight's words may be borrowed for an epitaph on such an ending—"She has become almost a divine or poetic principle."[8]

It is certainly true that at this point in the play Helena has been raised on to a pedestal—her virtue irradiates the scene at court.

It is equally true that, as Wilson Knight says, the play is "saturated
with religious thought and language". He is prompted to conclude
that "Helena functions as a bridge between religion and the court,
between humility and honour. In a world of divided, sin-struck
humanity she is a redeeming power, a perfect unit; that is her
function".[9]

As a description of the static symbolic reality of Helena, particularly as revealed in the post-healing scene, this seems fair, if a
shade over-enthusiastic. Moreover, such a view of Helena may be
corroborated when we recall the encomia spoken of her upon her
presumed death. Even Lavache, the cynic, refers to her as "the sweete
Margerom of the Sallet, or rather hearbe of grace".

Yet, however much part of our minds agrees with this, another
part finds it difficult to square it up with other features of Helena's
presence in the play. One man, and one man alone—Bertram—is
the catalyst which stirs us to see more than this static Helena and,
by implication, to move her into a different dimension of dramatic
reality.

Through healing the King, she achieves a status far transcending
her actual social position—which had so worried her previously.
Yet a view such as Wilson Knight's seems to ignore the fact that
the attainment by Helena of this new status is attempted for one
reason alone—to gain Bertram. All the transfiguration in heaven
or the world could not equal, for her, the kind of acceptance she
really desires. The ironic truth is that in the great "annunciation"
scene, as Helena climbs the pinnacle of admiration, one voice
pushes the play back on to its original course.

> I cannot love her, nor will strive to doo't.
>
> [II. III. 145]

Bertram will not marry a physician's daughter, earthly angel
though she may have become, and that is the fine of it. G. K.
Hunter confronts the difficulty which the audience has to face in
judging Helena's actions after Bertram's rejection.

> She expiates her "ambitious love" by abandoning worldly
> position, and her journey to Great St Jaques (via Florence) is

said unequivocally in the play to be a journey of contrition and
abrogation:

"death . . . I myself embrace to set him free."

and is accepted as such by the Countess and the two
Gentlemen, whose comments seem to reflect a norm
Shakespeare intends us to accept.

But can we accept this norm? Hunter pauses on this point.

> Of course there are difficulties in the way of this view. In her
> conversations with the Widow Helena appears as a schemer,
> and the reader may well feel that no single view of her
> conduct is possible.[10]

Helena appears to the Widow as a "holy pilgrim". She tells her her
secret. The Widow says she does not want to become involved in
any "staining act". Helena persuades her to help—saying that she
will not be guilty of any crime, since Bertram is her husband.
Helena explains her scheme.

> The Count he woes your daughter,
> Layes downe his wanton siedge before her beautie,
> Resolve to carrie her: let her in fine consent
> As wee'l direct her how 'tis best to beare it:
> Now his important blood will naught denie,
> That shee'l demand: a ring the Countie weares,
> That downward hath succeeded in his house
> From sonne to sonne, some foure or five discents,
> Since the first father wore it . . .
>
> [III. VII. 17–25]

The Widow replies,

> Now I see the bottome of your purpose.

Helena's explanation of the lawfulness of her plan seems curiously
chop-logic'd.

> Why then to night
> Let us assay our plot, which if it speed,
> Is wicked meaning in a lawfull deede;

And lawfull meaning in a lawfull act,
Where both not sinne, and yet a sinfulle fact.
[III. VII. 43–7]

The words themselves, one might say, add up to a theorem of
awfulness, but the glib deviousness of their expression does nothing but convince the audience that this is verbiage disguising conscience.

The bed-trick is the result of the "negotiations" with the
Widow. Doubtless, as Hunter points out, "There was little sense
among Shakespeare's contemporaries that this was a degrading
and unsatisfactory way of getting a husband, either in real life or
on the stage", yet, equally, "The psychological reality of Helena
and the realism of the background make the facile substitution of
one body for another seem irrelevant and tasteless".[11]

Indeed—what has happened to our angel? The truth is that
Helena, having been raised in the centre of the play to a symbolic
level where "grace", "love", and "virtue" co-mingle, has now
become a woman of physical appetite; fierce active desire has
taken the place of inert virtue. She has, in fact, reverted to what
she was at the beginning—slightly desperate, expedient, willing to
buy love. The effect on us is as if Portia had covertly directed
Bassanio to the right casket, or as if Viola had persuaded Olivia
to feign love for Orsino, and substituted herself in his bed. A sense
of fitness is destroyed. The result of Helena's enforced actions is to
cast doubt on the validity of the play's very title—will love so
bought be well? Moreover, her character is diminished in the sense
that we are now more convinced of the appetites of her love
rather than of its truth. The angelic Helena, the redemptive force,
is, after all, a woman who wants her man.

The dichotomy thus presented in Helena is present (in an
extreme form) in Bertram. Quite simply, we are asked by this
play to find him both acceptable and unacceptable. He "stands
for" the admirable young courtier-type; he is "virtuous" in the
sense of military virtue; he is "honourable" in seeking martial
glory; he is patently aristocratic. He is a younger Coriolanus,
brought up to fixed conventional standards of attitude and

behaviour. To this extent he is the embodiment of an abstraction—
the accepted Elizabethan courtier. Yet, he is much else. He is a
"Proud, scornfull boy", a "rash and unbridled boy". He is susceptible to bad influence, and can be "foolish and idle".

All these descriptions could be contained, in a way, within the
elastic notion of the admirable young courtier—the apprentice
nobleman—without destroying the ideal. Yet Bertram's
conventional nobility, honour, and virtue are completely
overshadowed by his priggishness, insensitivity, and deceit.
We find it no excuse that he has been brought up to a certain
sense of class, and that marriage to Helena would constitute a
slight to his high birth. We find it difficult to believe that his
behaviour, his cast of mind, is dictated entirely by the malevolent
influence of Parolles. The influence exists, but does not fully
account for the inner qualities of this young man. The explanation
is that Bertram, as a mechanical agency, is essential to the
plot-line; as a personality he is almost irrelevant. As Hunter
says,

> . . . he is not the central character; he illustrates ideas and
> tendencies that the play develops elsewhere and in other
> (sometimes more striking) ways.[12]

These are best developed in the character of Parolles. For all the
wayward eccentricities of the production, Sir Tyrone Guthrie's
interpretation of the play at the Shakespeare Memorial Theatre in
1959 was notable for the way in which it "fixed" the nature of
Parolles. He was a cross between mercenary soldier and dirty-
mouthed braggart. He haunted the rear of any battlefield picking
up largesse and repaying it with reckless gossip and lewd *bonhomie*.
He was, as played by Paul Hardwick, the most instinctive coward.
He is, in fact, the most carefully and consistently drawn character
in the play, but it is important to realise that all his characteristics
do not add up to a credible creature who can positively incite either
our pity *or* our admiration. In a sense we have no point of view on
Parolles; we know what he is from the outset—a collection of
follies and vices—but we are not required to do more than note
how predictable his actions and words are; this, however, is not to

say that we are not caught up with them as they appear. He is, indeed, in Lafeu's words, "muddied withal".

Yet he plays an important rôle in the play. It is through Parolles that we learn to regard, with some cynicism, the brave announcements about honour, chivalry, bravery, which are an integral, if standardised, part of Bertram's make-up. The emptiness of these concepts is more vividly embodied by Parolles than by Bertram, who lives in his shadow. Like Falstaff, Parolles sees through (in part himself helps to corrupt) the images of honour, bravery, and virtue. Unlike Hal, Bertram does not learn anything of human value from what he sees and hears. Both he and Parolles are oddly empty figures—they wear all that there is of them upon their sleeves. In Parolles's case we have no compulsion to explore what is underneath; in Bertram's case not only do we know that we will find nothing there, but that this knowledge, in itself, turns awry all our feelings about the play and its meaning.

Because Bertram and Parolles are thus, the case of Helena becomes more equivocal. The dialogue about virginity, at the outset, is, for Parolles, a playful, cynical, witty demonstration of lewd appetite. His words are not really directed to a particular person or set of circumstances; they are, more, an emblem of the lewd man who speaks them. It is this man to whom Bertram has become a dupe. Yet, it is towards Bertram that Helena's reflections on virginity are directed. And Bertram's dialogue with Diana, for all its fine phrases, is no less appetite-ridden than Parolles's.

> Stand no more off,
> But give thy selfe unto my sicke desires,
> Who then recovers. Say thou art mine and ever
> My love as it beginnes, shall so persever.
> [IV. I. 34–7]

He speaks to a Lord about his night's business, ending with a reference to his bedding of Diana—

> I meane the businesse is not ended, as fearing to heare of it hereafter.
> [IV. III. 91–2]

—which is as much as to say, "I've bedded her, told her I'll marry her; I hope she doesn't hold me to it."

Helena, then, is partly surrounded (and her eventual actions are governed) by attitudes which render entirely cynical the near-angelic status to which she was raised, and from which she has such a fall. She is more sinned against than sinning, but the pitch of Parolles and Bertram has defiled her nature and made sourly ironic her quest for the fulfilment of a particular love.

Yet the play has, deep in its centre, one character whose presence not only casts a sour look upon love but upon life itself. This is Lavache, described as Clown but who is, in fact, the least clownish of all Shakespeare's Fools. He is called "A shrewd knave and an unhappie". This is meticulously accurate. He is very much the observing and commenting wearer of motley, but his cynical view of the world is almost completely unmitigated by the tradi-tional leavening of zany wit which usually characterises the Fool figures. Even Lear's Fool has more in him of "court entertainer" than Lavache. Hardly anything he says is uncomplicated, in the sense that his verbal responses to particular circumstances always bear with them a double-meaning, or imply a half-mocking, half-cynical conception of life which is dominated by a kind of dis-missive despair. He is a very obvious example of the cynic who knows the price of everything and accepts the value of practically nothing. The only really warm sentiment he expresses is his remark about Helena's "grace".

In a very certain sense, then, Lavache's presence and personality confirm an impression of the uneasy cynicism which lurks about the play. Yet, more than this, he establishes a connection between the mood and spirit of this play and of *Troilus and Cressida*. In that play one of the most insistent features is the contrapuntal effect of opposites—true love and false love, true honour and false honour, high political theory and mean practice. It is remarkable that so many of Lavache's remarks and speeches display a similar play of opposites or, at times, a cancelling out of positive assertion by negative assertion, so that the final communication becomes a nothing. G. K. Hunter's comment on Lavache sums up precisely his position in the play:

Few, moreover, of the ideas with which the play is
concerned pass without derogatory comment from Lavatch;
he sees courtliness as a verbal trick, war as a shirking of
responsibility, greatness as an obedience of the devil.[13]

There is one aspect which, in itself, might be regarded as a mitigation of the implicit and explicit cynicism of the rest. The Countess
(a woman with Volumnia's strength of character but with an
infinitely finer tact), the King, and Lafeu have grace of spirit,
gentility of demeanour, kindness of disposition, and a grave and
pleasing wisdom. They seem, very much, to belong to an older
and different world from the others—one whose values are more
certain, both in conception and execution. Indeed, part of the
initial "charm" of Helena is derived from her association with
these people, and from their glowing report of her. There is no
doubt that much of the wisdom she displays, the grace she has,
seems the result of her own quite unequivocal recognition of the
values of this other world—at least at first. For, as Hunter says,
"Helena, no less than Bertram, has to forget her father and abandon her foster-mother the Countess, as he has to abandon his
mother and his foster-father the King."[14] This necessary abandon-
ment of the old world coincides with her entry into the new,
younger world, whose values are directed less by principle than by
expediency; it also coincides with her loss of the audience's total
sympathy. The old world of the play is not represented as defeated;
rather it seems tired, almost reaching the point of immobility. For
this reason its values seem less active than passive and, though their
presence cannot be overlooked, nor their potential influence
rejected, they exist largely as a kind of nostalgia. In dramatic
terms, they do not strikingly affect the movement of the play's
theme and action.

This play, then, is puzzling to the sensibilities. It is compact of
cynicism, satire, wisdom, sadness, fleeting gaiety. It is not, by any
means, desperately pessimistic, nor does it entirely dismiss optimism. It does, however, deny its title—all's well that ends well. The
words of the King come nearer to its mood. He says, at the end,

"All yet seems well." It is in all the implications of "seems" that
our problem, as an audience, lies.

Measure for Measure

The mood in which Shakespeare wrote *Troilus and Cressida* and
All's Well was still present when, some time in 1604, he committed *Measure for Measure* to paper. This, in itself, is sufficient to
justify a grouping together of these three plays. Matters of import
concerning the world, man and his usages, had turned sour on
him, as this play, no less than the other two, shows. What is most
remarkable is that during the period 1600 to 1606 he was also
writing, or in process of conceiving, other plays (the great tragedies) which, dark as is their picture of humanity's ways and means,
still powerfully convey a sense of man's innate nobility.

There is nothing noble in *Measure for Measure*—the "good"
characters, including Isabella and the Duke, leave us with a taste
of dissatisfaction at the contradictions which exist between their
principles and their practice. The tying up of knots at the end is
done with fingers that are theatrically dextrous but which have
lost touch with dramatic logic. In short, there is a credibility gap in
the play between the moral issues that are raised and their resolution in acceptable human terms. This makes us wary in something
like the way in which we are wary of some of Shaw's plays, where
he raises issues of moment only to seem to mock them.

The Duke is a case in point. He is, in the end, the one who
pardons from his magisterial height and dispenses judgement "like
power devine". Yet his actions are full of inconsistencies which
suit ill with such a station. He gives up his place to Angelo, leaving
us with a conspicuous feeling that he has decided to leave a mess
for someone else to clear up; his action in forcing Angelo to
marry Mariana, and then threatening to execute him, smacks of
sadism; in the theatre his sudden request to Isabella for her hand in
marriage matches Orsino's sudden decision to jump on the marital
band-wagon in *Twelfth Night*, but in this latter case Viola has completed, by now, her magical work of reconciling the disparate
elements in Illyria.

We find Isabella's conduct no less puzzling and irritating. She is a woman of great courage, intellectual subtlety and apparent moral strength; yet it is precisely the "apparent" which is worrying. The Elizabethan audience may very well, as W. W. Lawrence points out, have been far less squeamish than we are about, for example, Isabella's easy agreement to the Duke's plan to substitute Mariana for herself in Angelo's bed. He writes:

> The point of importance to keep in mind is the relation between Angelo and Mariana. The fact that they had earlier been affianced is of the utmost significance in drawing conclusions as to the morality of the story.[15]

In considering Isabella's actions in the light of her novitiate as a nun, Lawrence continues:

> An Elizabethan audience was not likely to be scandalised by the heroine's leaving a convent. . . . . Small niceties of ecclesiastical infringement were not shocking to Protestant England in Shakespeare's day.[16]

The generalisation about "Protestant England" itself begs many questions, but, in any case, one wonders why Shakespeare bothered to stress Isabella's addiction to the sisterhood, if he did not want to make some dramatic capital out of what Lawrence calls "niceties of ecclesiastical infringement". Whether Lawrence is right or not about the Elizabethan reception of Isabella, the truth is that the modern audience cannot swallow completely the several inconsistencies in her character. It finds itself asking disturbing questions about her. Why, for example, should Shakespeare have emphasised Isabella's desire to have even stronger restraints in the sisterhood if he did not, at one stage at least, want her to be presented as being most severely moral and pure? Surely one who looks for more restraints is not going to regard the substitution of herself by another in a man's bed as an irrelevant nicety? The twentieth century cannot fully accept Isabella as being blameless and morally perfect. There is a shadow across her name.

Some critics have tried to reconcile the irreconcilable elements in the characters by claiming that the play is a comedy. R. W. Chambers goes so far as to refer to it in these words:

> Shakespeare's audience expected a marriage at the end; and, though it may be an accident, the marriage of Isabel and the Duke makes a good ending to a Christmas play.[17]

One wonders whether even an Elizabethan audience, in the festive mood Chambers suggests, would have found that the whole play satisfied an appetite for lightheartedness and laughter. The "low-life" scenes and characters certainly would have satisfied such an audience; it might also have found the implied satire on the law and those who practise it appealing to its sense of humour; it might have found cause for wry smiling in the bed-trick. Yet what kind of comedy is it that has such scenes as the confrontations between Isabella and Angelo, such severe moral arguments upon whose resolution lives depend, such terrifying verbal realisations of the horror of death, and such an underswell of cynicism?

If this play be a comedy, then surely the same designation could be applied to a play in which a man is tricked into murder by a handkerchief and by palpably false reports of a kind that only a child might accept without question. The judgement of T. M. Parrott[18] comes nearest to expressing the uneasy status of this play. He writes of the ". . . incongruity between the tragic theme, the tragi-comedy technique and the realistic background."

Like *The Merchant of Venice*, *All's Well*, and *Troilus and Cressida*, the play perplexes, even irritates, our sense of fitness, while at the same time it is thoroughly satisfying as a piece of theatre. It is its theatrical power which commands attention even while we may regret its unpleasing inconsistencies of motivation, action, principle and practice.

The heart of the play's theatrical and dramatic potency is in the two scenes of confrontation between Isabella and Angelo (Act Two, scene two and Act Two, scene four). In no other play does Shakespeare demonstrate, at such length and concentration, his skill in writing dramatic, dialectic language. George Bernard Shaw could well have mitigated some of his less responsible remarks about Shakespeare if he had reflected more closely upon these scenes. But apart from his admiring remarks on the characterisation of Lucio in a review in 1898, he said little about the play; what he did say does not suggest a very precise application of thought to it.

> I read *Measure for Measure* through carefully some time ago with some intention of saying something positive myself; but its flashes of observation were so utterly unco-ordinated and so stuck together with commonplaces and reach-me-downs that I felt the whole thing would come to pieces in my hand if I touched it; so I thought it best to leave it as he left it, and let the stories and the characters hide the holes in the philosophic fabric.[19]

The scenes between Isabella and Angelo out-Shaw Shaw in their brilliant display of argument in dramatic form. Like Shaw at his best, as in the scenes between Warwick and the French in *St Joan*, Shakespeare has solved the problem of presenting thesis and anti-thesis without losing a grip on the need to provide dramatic interest and a sense of action. Psychological tension, the ebb and flow of emotional and intellectual responses, are both implicit and explicit in these two scenes. Even as one reads the text it is possible to feel and to visualise the human drama that is taking place. In Act Two, scene two, Angelo, at first, hardly notices Isabella; her carefully worded statements, models of logic, are punctuated by his short, sharp, peremptory phrases.

> Well, what's your suite.
>
> Well: the matter?
>
> Maiden, no remedy.
>
> Hee's sentenc'd, 'tis too late.
>
> Pray you be gone.
>
> [II. II. 29–62]

As Angelo becomes more dismissive, so Isabella's speeches become more emotionally charged. She moves from the plain urgency of,

No ceremony that to great ones longs,
Not the Kings Crowne; nor the deputed sword,
The Marshalls Truncheon, not the Judges Robe
Become them with one halfe so good a grace
As mercie does.

[II. II. 59–63]

to the penetrating passion of:

Why all the soules that were, were forfeit once,
And he that might the vantage best have tooke,
Found out the remedie: how would you be,
If he, which is the top of Judgement, should
But judge you, as you are? Oh, thinke on that,
And mercie then will breathe within your lips
Like man made new.

[II. II. 73–9]

Shakespeare is unerring in his psychological exactitude. At the
point where Isabella's words involve Angelo personally and she
turns from abstract argument into the particularity of the judgement, he looks at her, we believe, for the first time. His early
address—"Maiden, no remedy"—changes to—"Be you content,
fair maid." That word "fair" signifies the depth of his looking.
It is the fuse which, later, will explode his passion. From this point
onwards in the scene he argues with her with respect and with a
recognition of her intellectual equality. Yet the word "fair" has
stuck in his mind. He cannot argue with her so closely without
looking upon her closely. He begins to find that he cannot separate
her intellectual from her sexual power:

She speaks, and 'tis such sence
That my Sence breeds with it.

[II. II. 141–2]

The scene is a masterpiece of dramatic subtlety and dramatic
truth. It is also remarkable in its careful avoidance of a merely
simple kind of seduction. Isabella does not exert an explicit
sexual pressure, but her pressure brings about a vast change

in Angelo. The tone on which the scene ends is one of subtle irony. Angelo, who cannot be corrupted by evil, is tempted by goodness.

> Most dangerous
> Is that temptation, that doth goad us on
> To sinne, in loving vertue.
>
> [II. II. 181–2]

The arguments that each puts to the other concerning justice, mercy, and the law, take second place, in the theatre, to the intensity of the human situation which develops and to the irony which is involved. Shakespeare, we might say, passes through dialectic and achieves dramatic truth.

The second main confrontation between the two is no less dramatic. In terms of response from one to the other their rôles, at first, are reversed from the earlier meeting. At the beginning it is Angelo who is making propositions and statements, and Isabella who interrupts with short phrases. Whereas formerly it was Angelo who did not accept Isabella's arguments, now it is she who, impatient for a conclusion, is peremptory.

> 'Tis set downe so in heaven, but not on earth.
>
> How say you.
>
> So.
>
> True.
>
> [II. IV. 49–87]

The shift from theoretically presented case to personal issue again appears. Just as, previously, Isabella has slowly involved Angelo in her arguments about law and mercy so, now, she finds herself enmeshed in Angelo's question—"what would you do?" He has pressed her to make a personal decision about her reactions if the only way to save her brother is by laying down the treasures of her body. By the end of this second meeting the two are inextricably and personally involved in issues which began as abstractions.

As has been mentioned, it is the spectacle of human tensions

which grips us in the theatre—the issues remain secondary. Nevertheless they have some effect on the drama that is presented to us.
If we take them on their face value a simple equation can be made.
The Duke represents wisdom and mercy; Isabella represents chas-
tity unwilling to compromise even to save a brother's life;
Angelo represents law untouched by mercy. If we remain within
abstractions, what happens in the play is the triumph of mercy and
forgiveness over human weakness and corruption. As has frequently been pointed out, the play, with its title taken from the
gospels, concerns itself with the idea—"Judge not that ye be not
judged". This is the main issue, and we are aware, as the play proceeds, of the intricate variations that are being made upon it. But
over and above this awareness is a much stronger and prevailing
sense that Shakespeare is less interested in thesis drama than in
revealing the unreliability of human response when faced with
matters which ask for a direct moral decision. Thus the Duke is in
fact more memorable as a somewhat lazy, bumbling, self-indulgent autocrat than as a symbol of mercy and wisdom. Angelo
engages us less as an example of legal severity untempered by
mercy than as a weak man whose latent lasciviousness catches up
with him. Isabella's innocence is, as it is revealed, a pliable thing.
She is not far from being a priggish, holier-than-thou virgin, given
to somewhat tendentious sermonising:

> Take my defiance,
> Die, perish: Might but my bending downe
> Repreeve thee from thy fate, it should proceede.
> Ile pray a thousand praiers for thy death,
> No words to save thee.
>
> [III. I. 144–8]

Our sympathies do not go out to those three who, on face value,
represent a triangle of moral tensions; rather we are more drawn
to those who are affected by the triangle. Claudio, Lucio, and the
crew of bawds have the virtue of directness even if they are morally guilty of one crime or another. Simply speaking, they seem
more "honest" than the holy three. They do not wrap up their
beliefs or motivations in precepts which are denied by their

actions. Claudio merely wants to love and to live; Lucio, no less direct in his aspirations, is curiously honest about his time-serving occupation. He pretends to no other thing than to be an intelligent, witty bawd. After we have spent some time with Angelo, the Duke, and Isabella, we are even more inclined to say—why should those others not be what they either are or wish to be, for they have made no bones about the manner of their living. What Nosworthy says of Lucio may serve to stand for the rest of the low-life characters.

> He speaks scarely one word true throughout the play,
> and yet his lies and distortions shape themselves into a kind
> of truth.[20]

The "truth" of Lucio and his fellows is a kind of transparent honesty to their own iniquities. The lies and distortions are not hidden from us; we know, at each point of reference, when they are being expressed. For this reason Lucio and the others bring a refreshing air of realism and, paradoxically, non-equivocation into the play.

Lucio is more than a simple carrier of news and a tricksy leader of the low-life community. He has a little of Mercutio's bragga-docio attractiveness, and although his dexterity with words does not extend to lyrical fantasy, he has a similar witty incisiveness of speech, which is characterised by punning and an exquisite sense of the humour of sound.

> Some report, a Sea-maid spawn'd him. Some, that he was
> begot betweene two Stock-fishes. But it is certaine, that
> when he makes water, his Urine is congeal'd ice, that I
> know to bee true: and he is a motion generative, that's
> infallible.
>
> [III. II. 100–4]

Lucio stands, to some extent, in a parallel relationship to the Duke in the different societies which they overmaster. He is as assiduous in his championship of the unlawful as the Duke eventually is of the lawful. He has a very clear idea of the situation—indeed much clearer than anyone else. He says, of the Duke,

It was a mad fantasticall tricke of him to steale from the
State, and usurpe the beggerie he was never borne to.

[III. II. 86-8]

In the first meeting between Isabella and Angelo, his asides form
a chorus which increases our sense of the critical urgency of the
argument that is taking place. His deep knowledge of commodity
and opportunity in human affairs gives him a sensitive ability to
know how far to press a claim. When Angelo says to Isabella,
"Well: come to me tomorrow", Lucio immediately says to her,
"Goe to: 'tis well; away". Nosworthy's remark that he rarely
speaks one word true but that what he says adds up to a kind of
truth is amply confirmed in the scene between him and the Duke
in disguise. He claims that the Duke "had Crochets" in him; he
"would be drunke too". He is completely reckless, since he is
unaware of the Duke's identity, in his insinuations about the
Duke's character. Yet inside the free-ranging devilry of his tongue,
we find matter to which we can only nod in acceptance.

I would the Duke we talke of were return'd againe: this
ungenitur'd Agent will un-people the Province with
Continence.

[III. II. 162-4]

Lucio, indeed, is a realist. He well knows that Angelo's inflexible
legality is at variance with the reality of human behaviour. When
he speaks of "mercy" it is not as an abstraction but as a practical
matter. The Duke, whom he says he loves because of his imperfec-
tions, showed, he says, mercy to transgressors because "he had
some feeling of the sport, hee knew the service, and that instructed
him to mercie".

This is a different version of mercy from that exerted by the
Duke, which has the quality of an indulgence he can minister from
on high. In the long run Lucio's conception of mercy is seen as not
only more practical but more compassionate. Even though the
Duke, in the end, shows mercy and forgiveness, he seems at the
same time to be making up for his past laxness by attaching severe
penalties to his act.

Lucio's compassionate realism overrides, for us, his viler qualities of time-serving, lying, and supporting of the forces of unlawfulness, because it is more in keeping with the actualities of the society of Vienna. It is important to emphasise that Shakespeare gives us a brilliantly clear, detailed and naturalistic series of pictures of the low-life society of Vienna, whose flouting of the law has occasioned the Duke's decision to put affairs in the hands of Angelo. Nothing in the low-life scenes of *Henry IV*, or any other of the plays, approaches the stark naturalism of the Pompey/Overdone/Froth scenes in this play. We might, without fancy, conclude that they are the closest evocations of contemporary London low-life that Shakespeare created. When we read,

> If these houses have a box-brush, or an old post, it is enough
> to show their profession. But if they be graced with a sign
> complete, it's a sign of good custom. In these houses you
> shall see the history of Judith, Susanna, Daniel in the lions'
> den, or Dives and Lazarus painted upon the wall.[21]

it is the low life of *Measure for Measure* that we recall.

> *Pom.* Yonder man is carried to prison.
> *Mrs. Ov.* Well: what has he done?
> *Pom.* A Woman.
> *Mrs. Ov.* But what's his offence?
> *Pom.* Groping for Trowts, in a peculiar River.
> *Mrs. Ov.* What? is there a maid with child by him?
> *Pom.* No: but there's a woman with maid by him.
> [I. II. 82–8]

The sharp reality of these scenes, coupled with the function of Lucio, has a deep effect on our conception of what the play is saying to its audience. By comparison with the low-life characters, the upper-class society, despite its asseverations about justice, mercy and the law, never seems to get to grips with the reality of the situations it has to face. The resolutions of these situations are achieved by mechanistic means. "Justice" and "mercy" are bandied about, but, in the event, it is the imposed "accidents" of plot which resolve the issues. What they may mean or ought to mean in practice is more clearly shown through Lucio and through the realistic low scenes. What Shakespeare seems to be saying in this play is that justice and mercy as abstractions run the risk of being confounded by action; that the law as a mere concept is an ass, and that the dispensing of justice and of mercy must always be temporised by a recognition of the true nature of humankind. It is necessary to accept that man is imperfect, for, in this world,

> There is scarse truth enough alive to make Societies secure,
> but Securitie enough to make Fellowships accurst: Much
> upon this riddle runs the wisedome of the world.
>
> [III. II. 212–14]

It is a realistic view, mordantly expressed by Shakespeare. It shows all human weakness in stark clear detail and it shows even human virtues as tainted. If this be comedy, it has some sickness upon it.

Troilus and Cressida

The problems about the dating and textual condition of *Troilus and Cressida* have to take second place to the perplexities which the play arouses as a piece for theatrical realisation. They may be connected, but it would be a doughty man who held that they were, and attempted to justify any connection. A play, probably Shakespeare's, was noted in the Stationers' Register on 7 Feb. 1603, "as yt is acted by my Lord Chamberlens Men". On 28 Jan. 1609, "A booke called the history of Troylus and Cressida" (certainly Shakespeare's play) was licensed, and the quarto to which the licence applied was issued in the same year. The original title page was changed before publication and the lines "As it was acted by the Kings Majesties servants at the Globe" omitted. There was an addition to the effect that this was "a new play, never stal'd with the Stage", and describing it as the wittiest of Shakespeare's comedies.

In 1623 the play was included in the Folio, and its position there formerly raised some speculations that the editors were not quite certain whether to designate it as a comedy, a tragedy, or even a history. Twentieth-century scholarship, however, has established that it was intended to be placed after *Romeo and Juliet* amongst the tragedies, but that after three pages had been printed, for some reason the work on the play stopped and was not continued until the whole collected work was almost completed. *Troilus and Cressida* therefore appears between the histories and the tragedies.

The first recorded performance was during the Restoration. Dryden's version, *Troilus and Cressida, or Truth Found too late*,[22] displaced the original in the late seventeenth century and held sway until 1734. After this date there is no record of Shakespeare's original being performed until 1907. The later part of the twentieth century has dealt, statistically, more kindly with the play. It is now no longer the pariah it obviously was in the Shakespearean repertory, though the immense variety of contemporary stage interpretations is a telling proof that no solution to the play's basic problem has been found. The problem remains—is it comical satire or cynical tragedy? Theatre productions of the 1960s, so amenable to both controlled and self-indulgent experimentation, have attempted, from time to time, to reconcile comic and tragic, satirical and cynical. Some contemporary directors have been emboldened by the modish successes of absurdist dramatists. If life is meaningless and God is dead, traditional values become supernumerary, indeed a little eccentric. Tragic and comic become almost the same thing. To cry or to laugh, to fear or to rejoice, are merely responses which a dramatist may evoke, variations which have no meaning beyond their mere appearances. *Troilus and Cressida*, which has always been a particular problem as regards its mode, tone and effect, has been particularly susceptible to the post-war Western attitude of mind which (sometimes with arrogance) has assumed that it can solve or reconcile matters which have remained asunder over centuries of civilisation. Thus, the play, in production, has been used (notably by John Barton[23] in 1968) as a kind of set-piece confirmation of how possible it is to make Shakespeare speak to the twentieth century. In the hands of a director determined to show it as an image of our time, the play seems to reflect much that seems typical of ourselves. Political theory and practice are shown, cynically, at odds with one another; romantic love is at the mercy of sexual permissiveness;

honour in personal and public action is riddled with expediency. What we witness in *Troilus and Cressida*, so the modern director tells us, is a world which has lost its belief in a moral order. There is little sense that God or Gods exist in the heavens—time, rather than embodied fate and destiny, is the *deus ex machina* of the play.

The last few words spoken by the Prologue sum up the mood of "take it or leave it" which seems to have dominated Shakespeare while he was writing the play.

> Like, or finde fault, do as your pleasures are,
> Now good, or bad, 'tis but the chance of Warre.
>   [Prologue. 30–1]

Yet, there is a paradox here. The dominant mood is inescapable, but it has obviously had no enervating effect upon Shakespeare's imaginative power and dramatic skill. There are scenes of great emotional, dramatic and intellectual power. There are a number of characters who have been created with energetic subtlety. We seem to be in the presence not of a tired dramatist, but of one whose unabated skill is being used to communicate a vision of existence which has become sour and cynical. Dover Wilson encourages us to keep "a satiric purpose in mind" when we assess the play. He says that it amounts to an anatomising of the folly of both the Greeks and the Trojans. This advice cannot be ignored for, at every turn of the play, we find examples of a pointed satiric purpose—there is unconscious irony in Pandarus's warning to Troilus of the dangers of "mad idolatry" and again in the condescension of Hector's rebuke to Troilus and Paris a little later.

> For, after arguing in favour of the law of nature and of nations, which require the return of Helen, what he finally proposes is to keep her, "For it is a cause that hath no mean dependence/Upon our joint and several dignities." Here again, Shakespeare gives an ironic twist to his source by inventing a *volte-face* which makes Hector as vulnerable to satire as the thoughtless Troilus.[24]

If we accept the satiric purpose in the play, it is necessary to be clear about what is being satirised. There is nothing original in Shakespeare's depiction of the Troilus and Cressida story. He is not satirising it for its own sake; there would have been little need for him to do so, since Troilus, Cressida and Pandarus had been already firmly fixed in their symbolic rôles by earlier writers. Cressida was already synonymous with faithlessness, Pandarus with bawdry, and Troilus had taken up his position in romantic history as the employer of a bawd to ensure his liaison with Cressida.

Neither is Shakespeare's portrait of the other inhabitants of Greece and Troy uniquely pejorative. The status of those great heroes with reverberating names had declined greatly during the fifteenth century. Shakespeare had read Caxton's *Recuyell of the Historyes of Troy* (1475). This was itself based on an earlier medieval work—Guido delle Colonne's *Historia Troiana* (1287). What is common to most medieval writers on the legendary stories is the low opinion they held of the majority of the heroes. The Trojans are depicted as loose in behaviour, undisciplined in war, unamenable to reason. The Greeks (not least among them, Achilles) are a mob of brutes, bullies and fools.

Thus, neither in his treatment of the love plot nor of the legendary background, is Shakespeare original in the attitude he takes up, and the Elizabethan audience would not have been surprised by it. Yet, to regard the play simply as Shakespeare's satirical comment upon material which had already had its fair share of harsh and denigrating appraisal, is to deny the existence of a special potency. However much and often we warn ourselves of the danger of equating the imaginative worlds of Shakespeare's plays with the woof and warp of his own life, there are occasions when the warning is under siege. What, indeed, Shakespeare seems to be satirising with a ruthless force are many of those very themes and forms and attitudes which had created the life blood of his earlier plays. The noble conception of history, the sense of its awful sweep and depth are, in this play, reduced from a grand to a domestic architecture. It is with a sense of acute irony that we recall the Choruses of *Henry V* when we hear the Prologue to *Troilus and Cressida*:

> *To* Tenedos *they come,*
> *And the deepe-drawing Barke do there disgorge*
> *Their warlike frautage: now on Dardan Plaines*
> *The fresh and yet unbruised Greekes do pitch*
> *Their brave Pavillions.*
>
> [Prologue. 11–14]

The sense of diminution of history itself is all the more telling
since the *dramatis personae* of the play have names which, though
despoiled of reputation during the medieval period, still have
power to reverberate in the Western imagination—Hector,
Priam, Ulysses, Ajax. But history has become something from
which God, and the rhythms of fate and destiny, have been
removed, to be replaced by the notion of mere Time—an ill-
serving, mean-spirited, voracious consumer of men and their
deeds.

> Injurious time; now with a robbers haste
> Crams his rich theeverie up, he knowes not how.
> As many farwels as be stars in heaven,
> With distinct breath, and consign'd kisses to them,
> He fumbles up into a loose adiew;
> And scants us with a single famisht kisse,
> Distasting with the salt of broken teares.
>
> [IV. IV. 41–7]

The reduction of history is accompanied in the play by a demonstration of the collapse of the natural order which Shakespeare's
erstwhile conception of history implicitly involved. Ulysses's
speech on Degree has often been used by commentators as a set-
piece definition of the conception of order, and of the dangers
attending disorder, which lie at the basis of his history plays. There
is no need to deny the importance and the clarity of the speech in
this respect, while at the same time reflecting that, within the context of this play, the speech takes on a particular and ironic tone.
The speech is made in an atmosphere of empty pomp and circumstance. The great Greek leaders are met in council; they pay high-
sounding compliments to each other. "Great Agamemnon" is in

his "godly seat"; he is the "Nerve, and Bone of Greece"; Nestor is "venerable" and "most resolved"; Ulysses speaks "Most wisely". Yet there is something verging on the ridiculous behind all this. The studied formal gait of their language and what it communicates limps with rhetorical phrases.

> With due Observance of thy godly seat,
> Great *Agamemnon*, *Nestor* shall apply
> Thy latest words.
> In the reproofe of Chance,
> Lies the true proofe of men:
>   [I. III. 31–4]

Indeed Nestor's sententious phrase "In the reproofe of Chance, Lies the true proofe of men" is a sentiment straight out of Polonius's book of homilies. It is within an atmosphere of intellectual inertia and choked will that Ulysses makes the speech on Degree. The rest acknowledge its truth to their own situation, and ask what remedy his diagnosis suggests. Ulysses has spoken political philosophy; it is accepted as germane to the war, and yet, what follows? We hear of Achilles's "Lazy bed", of "Scurril jests", of undignified impersonations of the Greek leaders. We hear that Ajax is grown "self-willed", that there is a scabrous man called Thersites wandering about the Grecian tents. We learn that Hector is casting aspersions on Grecian womanhood and that, on this score, Nestor and Agamemnon himself are prepared to meet him in combat. In such a context, Ulysses's great speech seems an ironic irrelevancy. Such a situation, we might believe, hardly deserves consideration in the terms which Ulysses uses. He includes both the earth and the wide universe in his analysis of the nature of degree and order, but the application of the speech to Greece comes down to a lascivious, lazy warrior, his probably homosexual friend, to mockery of leadership, to self-conceit in a man of war, and a quarrel about whether Trojan women are superior to Greek. Shakespeare's English history plays have their ridiculous and petty incidents and characters, they have peevishness of motives, yet at no point is the great theme of order and disorder cheapened and by implication ridiculed. In this play Shakespeare,

D

apparently deliberately, has struck at the very heart of one of his most closely held and positive theses. He has satirised, we may feel, his own faith in a universal order.

This, however, is not all. The manner in which he deals with the story of Troilus and Cressida reveals him attacking another, most cherished, conception which had informed many of his earlier plays. It has been noted how a concern for order and disorder is manifest not only in the history plays, but in all the comedies—both the early ones and the mature ones that he wrote at a time very near to the writing of *Troilus and Cressida*. Love is enhanced, made valid and true by order, and is destroyed by disorder, which induces faithlessness and fickleness. All of Shakespeare's comedies up to this point have affirmed the validity of true love, governed by a correct ordering of the mind, the feelings, the spirit. In this play Shakespeare seems deliberately to concentrate on false love.

This has several aspects which revolve about the characters of Cressida, Troilus and Pandarus. It is tempting to speculate that Cressida at the age of thirty-nine would have many of the qualities of Livia in Middleton's *Women Beware Women*. Middleton's character delights in intrigue, but particularly that which involves sexual contest and deviousness. She is well aware of her own disposition, but her character is made up entirely of cunning and dangerous desire. Like Cressida she cannot be called completely wicked, since it is clear that she is a victim of her own self—she cannot help what she does.

> And if we lick a finger, then sometimes
> We are not too blame: Your best Cooks use it.[25]

A Cressida, having lost the bloom of youth both by age and the satisfaction of sexual desire, would we fancy, speak such words. She is a flawless beauty with the instincts of a whore. There is little point in seeking subtlety in her character, since Shakespeare has not endowed her with much emotional sensitivity or moral scruple. She has a bright and brittle intelligence, with Viola and Rosalind's skill in witty badinage but without their delicacy of spirit.

> *Cres.* Why *Paris* hath colour enough.
>
> *Pan.* So, he has.
>
> *Cres.* Then *Troylus* should have too much, if she pras'd him above, his complexion is higher then his, he having colour enough, and the other higher, is too flaming a praise for a good complexion, I had as lieve *Hellens* golden tongue had commended *Troylus* for a copper nose.
>
> [I. II. 95–101]

Her priorities of occupation are quite clear. When Pandarus says "A man knowes not at what ward you lye", she replies,

> Upon my backe, to defend my belly; upon my wit, to defend my wiles; uppon my secrecy, to defend mine honesty; my Maske, to defend my beauty, and you to defend all these.
>
> [I. II. 252–6]

Her sexuality is implicit from the very first, both in her unblushing responses to Pandarus's bawdry, and in her own language: "joyes soule lyes in the dooing"; "Men prize the thing ungain'd, more then it is"; "That she was never yet, that ever knew/Love got so sweet, as when desire did sue". Her sexuality is the more emphasised by her impersonation of coyness at the first meeting with Troilus. She has already told us, "That though my heart's Contents firm love doth beare,/Nothing of that shall from mine eyes appeare." So we may expect deception. When it comes it is precisely of that kind practised by the sexually devious female—a pretended reluctance.

> *Troy.* O *Cressida*, how often have I wisht me thus?
>
> *Cres.* Wisht, my Lord?—the gods grant? —
>
> O my Lord.
>
> [III. II. 59–60]

Her very nature prevents her from keeping up the act for long. She is soon tantalising Troilus with a curiously professional sounding assessment of sexual possibility.

> They say all Lovers sweare more performance then they are able, and yet reserve an ability that they never performe:

vowing more then the perfection of ten; and discharging
lesse then the tenth part of one.

[III. II. 81–4]

She follows this a little later by a further demonstration of her
ability at sexual titillation.

> *Troy.* What offends you Lady?
> *Cres.* Sir, mine owne company.
> *Troy.* You cannot shun your selfe.
> *Cres.* Let me goe and try:
> I have a kinde of selfe recides with you:
> But an unkinde selfe, that it selfe will leave,
> To be anothers foole. Where is my wit?
> I would be gone: I speake and know not what.
>
> [III. II. 140–7]

Her reiterated appeals to Troilus to "Be true" in the parting scene
before she is taken to the Greek camp, and her avowals of love
seem, in themselves, genuine enough, but Shakespeare does not
allow us to harbour for very long any idea that we may have
earlier misjudged her. The scene in which she is greeted with
kisses by the Greek commanders assures us that her previous protestations to Troilus are the spontaneous outbursts of a woman
who has been immensely satisfied in her sexual encounters with
him and who requires more. Her appeals for him to "Be true"
come to seem very much like the cry of the natural libertine who,
having given herself to a man, claims an exclusive possession of his
affections which, ironically, she herself is often the first to betray.
Ulysses has her measure exactly; the Cressida he describes is
exactly the Cressida who gradually unfolds herself in the play—a
beautiful harlot who will "Sing any man at first sight".

> Ther's a language in her eye, her cheeke, her lip;
> Nay, her foote speakes, her wanton spirites looke out
> At every joynt, and motive of her body:
> Oh these encounterers so glib of tongue,
> That give a coasting welcome ere it comes;
> And wide unclaspe the tables of their thoughts,

> To every tickling reader: set them downe,
> For sluttish spoyles of opportunitie;
> And daughters of the game.
>
> [IV. V. 55–63]

Cressida herself confirms Ulysses's judgement. She has no illusion about herself, but she attributes her failings to the infirmities of the female sex.

> The errour of our eye, directs our minde.
> What errour leads, must erre: O then conclude,
> Mindes swai'd by eyes, are full of turpitude.
>
> [V. II. 107–9]

By comparison with Cressida, Troilus seems a paragon of the romantic lover. He expresses himself with a fiery passion; his descriptions of Cressida take exaggerated flight. He is urgent in his pursuit of her love; her perfidy strikes him to the heart and his expression of grief is as profound as his protestations of love. Yet there is something about him that is unattractive. It is partly that he seems over-anxious, and therefore ludicrously emotional in praising Cressida (just as Romeo lays himself open to mockery in his exaggerated claims for Rosaline). What, however, makes Troilus unsympathetic is not entirely the result of his own personality, but also of the context in which his love is placed. His kind of young, urgent romanticism seems entirely out of key in a society which harbours expedient people like Diomed, sophisticated lovers like Helen and Paris, devious men like Pandarus and, above all, time-servers like Cressida. Love in this play is largely presented as a pawn in a political chess game and as a means of sexual satisfaction. Troilus's rarefied notions of love are entirely out of place here—he is made to look foolish because he is an outsider; his rightful place is the Forest of Arden, not these Trojan wars. Even his emergence as a powerful young commander towards the end of the play does little to alter the image that we retain of him. As Tillyard says,

> I fancy that one reason why the play fails to satisfy us
> completely is that Troilus as a character is made to bear too

much, that his double part of romantic and unfortunate
lover and of leading spirit among the Trojan commanders
taxes the spectator's aesthetic credulity beyond its powers.[26]

The force of the irony which Shakespeare has exerted upon the
love story of Troilus and Cressida is increased by the presence of
Pandarus. In the long run, the kind of love that Cressida is capable
of giving and the kind that Troilus requires are incompatible—the
expedient and the romantic do not make for permanent bed-
fellowship. None the less these two are brought together, and
by one who cannot have any conception of Troilus's notion of
love.

Pandarus does not stand for good sense and he does not
inhabit the same world as Troilus. He is good natured but
he is coarse; and the kind of love that possesses Troilus is
quite outside his experience or power of imagination.[27]

In these words Tillyard has indicated how absolute is the separa-
tion of Troilus and Pandarus. He has shown too that the separa-
tion is reflected in the opening scenes where Troilus speaks verse
and Pandarus prose. The difference is striking in effect.

> *Troy.* Still have I tarried.
> *Pan.* I, to the leavening; but heares yet in the word
>   hereafter, the Kneading, the making of the Cake, the
>   heating of the Oven, and the Baking; nay, you must stay
>   the cooling too, or you may chance to burne your lips.
> *Troy.* Patience her self, what Goddesse ere she be,
>   Doth lesser blench at suffererance, then I doe:
>   At *Priams* Royall Table doe I sit,
>   And when faire *Cressid* comes into my thoughts,
>   So (Traitor) then she comes, when she is thence.
>   [I. I. 20–31]

The truth is that Troilus is pushed even further out of our sympathies, and his kind of love seems even more incompatible with
Pandarus's and Cressida's because Pandarus is far more interesting
than Troilus. We cannot help ourselves wanting to hear the innu-

endoed cackling of this cunning old gossip; he has a far greater sense of humour, his intelligence is sharper, his attitude, if oiled with lechery, is more realistic than Troilus's. But the reduction of the romantic conception of love by irony and satire is intensified by the fact that there is such a consanguinity of spirit between Pandarus and Cressida. They are, basically, of the same breed, and are creatures of appetite. Cressida can match his innuendoes word for word, responds to the lascivious excitement of his verbal sexuality without demur. Troilus—and romantic love—are merely counters in the game which these two are playing.

There is no mitigation by Shakespeare of the judgement of Cressida which she forces upon us. The scene in which Troilus observes her and Diomed serves only to emphasise the kind of woman she is, and it harshly makes Troilus's romantic postures seem even more pathetically ludicrous. In this scene Cressida proves in action her own assessment that the weakness of woman is that "The errour of our eye directs our minde". Her feelings for Troilus take on the aspect of a kind of nostalgia which becomes mixed with her disposition to flirt and to yield to anyone.

> *Dio.* I doe not like this fooling.
> *Ther.* Nor I by *Pluto*: but that that likes not me, pleases me best.
> *Dio.* What shall I come? the houre.
> *Cres.* I, come: O *Jove*! doe, come: I shall be plagu'd.
> *Dio.* Farewell till then.
> *Cres.* Good night: I prythee come:
> *Troylus* farewell; one eye yet lookes on thee.
>
> [v. ii. 100–5]

Order and true love—the twin focuses of Shakespeare's vision of human existence—are thus smashed in this play. It is important to emphasise the extent of the destruction which he indulges in. Order, which involves honour, fidelity, chivalry, reason, grandeur of spirit, is comprehensively annihilated. In Achilles martial courage is seen as laziness, honour as treachery, nobility of spirit as lascivious hedonism; in Ajax soldierly strength is shown as brute, ignorant, conceited, physical strength. In Hector, even, chivalry is self-indulgent. Where love is concerned it is shown as false, blind, ministering to appetite, and its consummation served by lechery.

There are two particular characters whose presence and function suggest the depths of speculation and feeling out of which the play was born. The first is Thersites. One of the most significant things about this scurrilous, physically disgusting rag of a man is that he is well-known and, furthermore, the close acquaintance of so many of the characters. That he should be the confidant and acquaintance of men in high position is in itself a terrible reflection of the disease which Ulysses so eloquently diagnoses. His position among the Greeks is one of allowed vice. His presence adds to our sense of disorder and chaos a fog of disgust, darkening the dismal and pessimistic view of the world which the play reflects. Yet he is also used to specify and to confirm in detail all that we learn from the play's actions and characters. He is a Fool in the sense that he sees behind appearances, but he is less than Fool in that he is disgusting in himself, is rabidly committed to his own opinions and so lacks that curious objectivity which, in different degrees, makes Feste, Touchstone and Lear's Fool both mysterious and sympathetic. He is comprehensive in his indictment. He satirises Agamemnon, abuses Achilles and Patroclus, rails unmercifully at Ajax, knowing him for what he is; he tells us of Ulysses's and Nestor's mouldy wit, wishes the "bone-ach" on the whole camp—"For that me thinkes is the curse dependant on those that warre for a placket." He several times "sums up" the play—"Still warres and lechery, nothing else holds fashion. A burning divell take them."

Thersites, we may say, symbolises Shakespeare's pessimistic, dismissive, disgusted conclusions about the world. Yet in this respect, he is confronted by an opposing symbolism—that of Ulysses. It is worth noting that Agamemnon himself makes a direct contrast between Ulysses and Thersites.

> Speak Prince of *Ithaca*, and be't of lesse expect:
> That matter needlesse of importlesse burthen
> Divide thy lips; then we are confident,

When rank *Thersites* opes his Masticke jawes,
We shall heare Musicke, Wit, and Oracle.
                                        [I. III. 70–4]

It is Ulysses who comes nearest to occupying the status of the true
Fool in his rôle as a repository of wisdom. Ulysses, of course, does
not wear motley, but there is certainly none in his brain; he is not a
professional entertainer, though he has the power to command
listeners; he is not disconnected or incompletely connected to a
particular class in society, and yet the nature of his wisdom marks
him off from the others. He is Fool in the sense of Jaques's words:

> Give me leave
> To speake my minde, and I will through and through
> Cleanse the foule bodie of th'infected world,
> If they will patiently receive my medicine.
>   [*As You Like It*. II. VII. 58–61]

The Greeks do patiently listen to his medicine—he calls it himself
"Derision medicinable"—and it is acted upon, though not with the
results that are expected. He affirms order, though he knows it to
be gone; he knows the difference between true and false love; he
speaks about man's works and the operations of time with a grave
and wry wisdom. He is, in fact, as much of a realist as Thersites,
but with important differences. His realism is derived from a
positive view of the universe. He regrets the condition of the
world, but has lost no faith in what its true state should be. His
assessment of people is accurate (as in the case of Cressida) without being harsh; his wisdom is kindly. He is marked off from
Thersites as clearly as white is from black. He is the only character
in the play who upholds human dignity, both by being dignified
in himself, and through his words and deeds.

The question arises as to why such a positive and creative agent
is found in a play which so conspicuously paints a negative, anni-
hilative picture of the world. It may be suggested that he is a
powerful residue of that optimism which had previously governed
Shakespeare so certainly. Nothing can prevent us from taking
away with our experience of this play a sense of disillusion,

cynicism, irony and satire. Yet Ulysses remains as a reminder of the brighter times of Shakespeare's spirit and imagination and, significantly, as an earnest that there will be a return to them. Ulysses's wisdom, grave kindliness, insight and mysterious intuitiveness are not far removed from the qualities of certain characters in Shakespeare's last plays which affirm the return of Shakespeare's optimistic faith in human kind: in thinking of Ulysses we are perhaps dimly aware of the eventual approach of Prospero.

ill||||||||||||||||||||||||||||||||||||||||||||||||||||||||||||||||||||||||||||||||||||||||||||||||||||

4

ROME AND JULIUS CAESAR

The problems of the chronology of the plays between 1599 and 1608 are great and, in some cases, insoluble. One example alone (*Hamlet*) confirms the difficulties of assigning specific plays to particular years with any confidence. At least four different dates have been proposed, over the years, for *Hamlet*—1596, 1600, 1601 and 1603. Yet the mode and intention of some scholarship makes it crucial that the scholar should have come to a decision about the dating of the play. On the decision could depend the kind of answer given to basic critical questions, such as, "Does *Hamlet* precede or is it commingled with the writing of the so-called 'problem' plays?"

Julius Caesar, one of Shakespeare's most popular plays, is not immune from the problems. It has variously been assigned to 1599, 1600 and, less credibly, to 1607. What is crucial here is whether it precedes or follows *Hamlet*. Is it a link between the incipient tragedy of the "problem" plays and its full and awesome appearance in *Hamlet*? Does it follow, perhaps? Many scholars and critics have either noted or expatiated upon its apparently close affiliations with *Hamlet*. Mary McCarthy's description of Brutus might, without alteration, be attached to Hamlet:

> *Julius Caesar* is about the tragic consequences that befall
> idealism when it attempts to enter the sphere of
> action.[1]

Her words may be taken as an emblem of the many critical

accounts which have tied *Julius Caesar* very closely to *Hamlet* and firmly attached it to the world of the great tragedies.

Since the dating of *Hamlet* is uncertain, and likely to remain so, it is of little consolation to record that many recent scholars regard 1599 as the most likely date for the composition of *Julius Caesar*. This conclusion usually has, at its base, an account by a Swiss doctor, Thomas Platter, who visited London in 1599 and saw two plays. One is described in this fashion;

> After dinner on the 21 September, at about 2 o'clock, I went
> over the river with my companions, and in the thatched
> house saw the Tragedy of the first Emperor Julius Caesar,
> with at least 15 characters, acted very well.[2]

It is assumed that this refers to Shakespeare's play. It should also be recalled that Ben Jonson's *Every Man Out of his Humour*, entered in the Stationers' Register on 8 Apr. 1600, contains a possible reference to Shakespeare's play. In Act Five, scene two, there is the line "No, lady, this is a kinsman to Justice Silence"; in Act Three there seems to be an echo of the line in *Julius Caesar*—"O judgement, thou art fled to brutish beasts"—in "reason long since is fled to animals", though this may be quite coincidental. Whatever the truth of the chronological relationship of *Julius Caesar* to *Hamlet* or to any other play written in the period 1599 to 1605, there can be little doubt that there is a consanguinity between it and the tragedies, particularly *Hamlet*. Brutus's nature—whose inner complex is tested by outer circumstance to breaking point—easily recalls to the mind that of the great tragic protagonists. Again, there is the impression that a weakness, a corruption, having its source within men of power, can spread to destroy the society around them; this theme of proliferating disorder is as strong in *Julius Caesar* as in the tragedies. Thirdly, as in the tragedies to one degree or another, portents and apparently supernatural occurrences function as symbolic comments upon the action. Finally, and most obviously, Brutus has in large measure that introspection, containing a torturing self-knowledge, which is characteristic in varying degrees of the tragic protagonists, but particularly of Hamlet. Such words as these from Brutus

are closely akin to the self-analysing soliloquies of Hamlet the
Dane.

> Between the acting of a dreadfull thing,
> And the first motion, all the *Interim* is
> Like a *Phantasma*, or a hideous Dreame:
> The *Genius*, and the mortall Instruments
> Are then in councell; and the state of a man,
> Like to a little Kingdome, suffers then
> The nature of an Insurrection.
>
> [II. I. 62–9]

Indeed, it is not difficult to make out a strong case for this play
as a companion piece to the great tragedies. Yet there is much to
set against it. Firstly, though one may see the tension created
between the inner man and outward circumstances, this tension
has a good deal of slack in it. Brutus in his self-deliberations never
"follows-through" to such terrible and self-wounding conclusions
as does Hamlet or Macbeth. The tension, it may be said, is too
commonplace; it is a kind that we habitually believe to be present
in all men who have some goodness and conscience and yet are
involved in the equivocations of political action. In other words,
Brutus's personality lacks uniqueness in what it reveals to us of its
response to external events. Secondly, although the theme of disorder, of spreading corruption, is vividly, almost naturalistically,
presented to us, particularly in the scenes where the mob is on the
rampage, in a sense this also seems too ordinary, too expected.
We know from experience that social strife often follows political
assassination, that men will be killed and property destroyed. We
may marvel at Shakespeare's depiction of this but we do not, as in
Hamlet and *Macbeth*, shudder at the "unnaturalness" of it. In the
great tragedies nature itself seems disarrayed; in *Julius Caesar* it is
"merely" a particular society that is shaken. The supernatural elements have more of the character of personal superstition than of
mysterious portent—the other world does not surround Rome as
potently as it pervades Elsinore.

In the theatre *Julius Caesar* simply does not engage us as a
tragedy in the highest sense, though it has its own magnetism.

This has its source and power in the play's ability to seem (and, indeed, often to be) "contemporary". The play has, in successive decades, not only provided its readers with points of reference for an appreciation of contemporary political events, but has seemed particularly amenable to being presented in contemporary dress. From the 1940s, for example, the possibility of dressing and setting the play to align it to the Fascist world of the 1930s has proved too strong a temptation for a number of theatre directors.[3] Politics and political men have perhaps always, but most certainly in the twentieth century, been of high news-value, exerting a fascination which is compelling and unfailing. It is precisely this compulsion that the play exploits with such skill. More than this it gives us (particularly in the twentieth century) the kind of insight into the political world demanded by our curiosity and imagination. We are shown the inside workings as well as the outside configurations of that world; our view is double-focused. We are, for example, given glimpses of the reasons why Caesar held such sway, but these singularities are shown in parallel with other elements in him which are common and possessed by lesser and weaker men. Qualities he shares with some modern dictators, his courage, his bravura, his ability to command, his expectation of immediate obedience, his peremptory assumption of absolute authority, are shown. Yet we see also the pettiness of mind, the fears, the almost absurdly ordinary emotional response of the man. The contrast between public and private, between great singularity and petty plurality—these titillations of our curiosity about political men—is vividly presented. What Shakespeare has done is to encapsule it in a play of remarkable political and human insight.

If *Julius Caesar* counterpoints our own experience of the twentieth-century world of politics, it is surely not beyond possibility that for the Elizabethans (especially those who strode very near to the arass'd corridors of power) it came near to the quick of actual events in their own time. We can only guess what Elizabethan actualities lurk behind Shakespeare's rewriting of Roman history. How much of the Earl of Essex is in Brutus and what taffeta'd courtier is partly hidden behind Casius's thin smile? The questions are unanswerable, yet worth posing since they remind us that the kind of political and human insight revealed in the play could have been gained only by a man who had himself sat very near the seats of power. Shakespeare's literary sources gave him much, but what they could not give him was the ability to convey a sense of actuality and fidelity to political and human affairs; only keen and close observation could do that. The tense and quarrelsome meeting of Cassius and Brutus before Philippi is expressed thus in North's translation of Plutarch's life of Marcus Brutus.

> Therefore before they fell in hand with any other matter, they went unto a little chamber together, and bade every man avoid, and did shut the doors to them. Then they began to pour out their complaints one to the other, and grew hot and loud, earnestly accusing one another, and at length both fell a-weeping.[4]

In Shakespeare's play it is transmuted into this.

> *Cassi.* Most Noble Brother, you have done me wrong.
> *Brut.* Judge me you Gods; wrong I mine Enemies?
>   And if not so, how should I wrong a Brother.
> *Cassi.* *Brutus*, this sober forme of yours, hides wrongs,
>   And when you do them——
> *Brut. Cassius*, be content,
>   Speake your greefes softly, I do know you well.
>   Before the eyes of both our Armies heere
>   (Which should perceive nothing but Love from us)
>   Let us not wrangle.   [IV. II. 36–45]

Such scenes emphasise the quality of Shakespeare's intimate knowledge of the woof and warp of private and political. It also induces in the reader and the theatregoer the feeling,

>   Tut I am in their bosomes, and I know
>   Wherefore they do it.   [v. I. 7–8]

One of the most pressing questions aroused by the play is whether it enshrines or conveys a "political philosophy"—either as an implied set of principles or as a series of hints about Shakespeare's attitude to the rights and wrongs of political thought and action.

It is worth emphasising again that to ask such questions of creative artists is always tempting and always dangerous. The most that it is safe to do is to measure the drift of ideas in a particular work against the moving tide of all the author's works. On such a measurement *Julius Caesar* shows that Shakespeare's prevailing detestation of disorder, his celebration of order, his loathing of irrationality in thought and action, had not abated. The Boar's Head, the Courts of Richard of Gloucester, of Harry of Monmouth, of Bolingbroke, Richard II, Henry VI and, indeed, the Forest of Arden, are now joined by Rome as emblems of Shakespeare's view of what makes for good and bad societies.

What gives *Julius Caesar* such a sharpness of outline is the number of different ways in which the perils of disorder are displayed and manipulated. Each one of the characters—Caesar, Brutus, Cassius, Antony and Octavius Caesar, as well as the mob—is a distinct example of the incompatibility of political and private moralities. Dominating this incompatibility is the element of power, and the play may be said to demonstrate the corrosive effect of power on these men, ranging from the cold embrace of it by Octavius Caesar to Brutus's self-torturing attempts to allay its destructive force.

We see Julius Caesar himself after power has completed its work of raising the public man high at the expense of ruining the private man. It is on Caesar that Shakespeare exerts the fullest rigour of his bifocal view, showing us relentlessly the effortless, conceited, assumed public domination of the man and, at the same time, his pettiness. For most onlookers, though not for all, the public man is respected, not for his humanity, but merely for his power:

> Who else would soare above the view of men,
> And keepe us all in servile fearfulnesse.
>
> [I. I. 75–6]

When we first meet him it is as a public spectacle, surrounded by his courtiers and a great crowd. He is like some Eastern potentate, addressed with fulsome repetitiveness as Caesar, and who addresses himself in the third person. Shakespeare does not make the mistake of stating too violent a contrast between the image of public authority and the private man. Cassius's account of Caesar's physical weakness and fear when swimming the Tiber is prevented from destroying the first image by the envy in Cassius's tone:

> And this Man,
> Is now become a God, and *Cassius* is
> A wretched Creature, and must bend his body,
> If *Caesar* carelessly but nod on him.
>   [I. II. 115–18]

A generation which has lived through and remembers Hitler's Germany will perhaps be even less inclined to allow Cassius's innuendoes to diminish the power of Caesar's public image. Hitler's wounded arm, the shuffling leg, the hunted eyes which he was left with after the assassination attempt did not diminish the magnetism of his presence; the voice still hypnotised.

So is it with Caesar. In virtually the same breath Cassius refers to his "feeble temper" and to his bestriding the world "like a Colossus". The Caesar who is presented to us in this play is cast in an image which includes both strength and weakness—he has, as it were, both a good and a bad profile. The light which Shakespeare casts upon him from different angles gives us a constantly changing impression of the reality of the man.

Caesar's ability to assess those around him is peremptory but superbly accurate:

> Yond *Cassius* has a leane and hungry looke,
> He thinkes too much: such men are dangerous.
>   [I. II. 194–5]

His oracularly expressed stoicism seems natural, not assumed, yet there is a self-pride in it:

> It seemes to me most strange that men should feare,
> Seeing that death, a necessary end
> Will come, when it will come.
>   [II. II. 35–7]

His authoritarianism has a petulance about it:

> The cause is in my Will, I will not come,
> That is enough to satisfie the Senate.
>
> [II. II. 71–2]

Even this most obviously typical characteristic, egocentric
authority, seems a form of self-indulgence—his vulnerability to
believing what he wants to believe. He is taken in by Decius's
speciously flattering interpretation of a dream which his own
wife regards as ominous. His self-conscious assumption of the
mantle of Caesardom is, curiously, both dignified and slightly
absurd.

> But I am constant as the Northerne Starre,
> Of whose true fixt, and resting quality,
> There is no fellow in the Firmament.
>
> [III. I. 60–2]

Shakespeare gives Caesar one characteristic whose significance
has been consistently ignored by commentators on this play. Its
presence indicates, again, the shrewdness of his perceptiveness
about the political animal. Shakespeare was aware that the art of
politics involves histrionics—the most successful politician usually
turns out to be a consummate actor. In no other kind of politician is
there greater development of a sense of histrionics than in the
authoritarian/dictator type. We recall Hitler's "performances" in
his speeches, and the chin-thrusting, strutting and bellowing of
Mussolini; Napoleon stares out at us across the decades in countless
illustrations with a pose so theatrical in its hand-hiding that it has
become the symbol of sensational egomania. In the following
report there is a clear indication of Caesar's use of histrionics to
gain sympathy; he is utilising a disability for dramatic effect.

> Marry, before he fell downe, when he perceiv'd the common
> Heard was glad he refus'd the Crowne, he pluckt me ope
> his Doublet, and offer'd them his Throat to cut. . . . Three
> or foure Wenches where I stood, cryed, Alasse good Soule,
> and forgave him with all their hearts: But there's no heed to

be taken of them; if *Caesar* had stab'd their Mothers, they
would have done no lesse.

[I. II. 262–74]

We may recall, too, that Richard of Gloucester opened his doublet
and offered his bare chest. The occasion was different, but the
method and the intention were exactly the same. There is evidence
that Shakespeare consciously emphasised the histrionic quality of
Caesar's activities in this scene. By a slight departure from his
source in North's Plutarch he immensely increases the sense of the
theatrical in Caesar's behaviour. Plutarch has Caesar departing
"home to his house, and tearing open his doublet collar, making
his neck bare, he cried aloud to his friends that his throat was
ready to offer any man that would come and cut it". This is
dramatic enough but is presented to a limited audience—in a
private theatre, as it were. Its effect is as nothing compared with the
sensational theatricality of his doing it before a vast audience—it
out-Hollywoods Hollywood. Casca, who knows political men
and their ways, has the pith of it—"if the tag-ragge people did not
clap him, and hisse him, according as he pleas'd and displeased
them, as they use to do the Players in the Theatre, I am no true
man".

When this Caesar dies our emotions are extremely mixed. On
the evidence presented by the play his death seems unnecessary,
and yet when we consider the implications of the corrosive power
that dominates such men, his death seems a relief and is not sur-
prising. We are not sorry for Julius Caesar, neither are we completely glad. The likes of him fascinate our curiosities and turn awry
our judgements and our power to be sure of what we feel and
think. That is why they are so dangerous and so attractive.

Brutus could never become a Caesar because he is too honest a
man and incapable of play-acting. He is the Adlai Stevenson of
Rome. It is remarkable that, in a certain sense, we as listeners and
observers of Brutus lack confidence in him. His courage, his fidelity
to a cause, his intellectual and emotional honesty—none of these
are in doubt; yet we constantly doubt whether his heart is, and is
capable of being, committed to the pursuance of those actions

which will be necessary once he has thrown in his lot with the conspirators. We observed and listened to Stevenson as he set out on
his presidential campaigns and we applauded every example (and
there were many) of wisdom, honesty, integrity and sensibility.
Yet we had a strong sense that he was unequipped for the harsh
political world; in Stevenson, it seemed, the private, the human and
the personal were at odds with the public, the political, the expedient.

The effect of Brutus upon us is very similar. His purpose is
blunted. We observe him at various stages of the journey that
starts with Caesar's death and which ends at Philippi. It might
have ended back in Rome with laurel wreaths about his head, but
in our hearts we know all along that Philippi will be the end. The
fight between political necessity and personal sensibility atrophies
his well-meant intentions.

He is a man to whom introspection is natural and, we would
believe, is happiest when least in company. Then as he puts it,

> I turne the trouble of my Countenance
> Meerely upon my selfe.
>
> [I. II. 38–9]

He gives the impression that he is not a natural leader of active
opposition, least of all of the kind which will lead to assassination.
His observation of Caesar has caused him to reflect pessimistically
and to fear the direction which Caesar's rule is taking, but he has
to be cajoled into taking action. Although he says to Cassius,
"What you would work me to, I have some aim", we cannot really
believe that he would have contemplated assassination except as
an abstract solution. It has gone unremarked by most commentators that Brutus is finally pushed to commit himself to the
conspiracy by a cheap trick. The letters that Cassius throws through
his window are forged:

> I will this Night,
> In severall Hands, in at his Windowes throw,
> As if they came from severall Citizens,
> Writings, all tending to the great opinion
> That Rome holds of his Name:
>
> [I. II. 314–18]

Brutus's mind is made up for him by a deception.

> Am I entreated
> To speake, and strike? O Rome, I make thee promise,
> If the redresse will follow, thou receivest
> Thy full Petition at the hand of *Brutus*.
>
> [II. I. 55–8]

The effect of our knowing that they are forgeries is, or should be, twofold. First, that Brutus should be thus deceived increases our sense of his vulnerability in the harsh political world; second, that he should so quickly respond to them initiates a conviction in us that he is politically naïve. From the moment of the delivery of the letters Brutus's vulnerability and political insufficiency are emphasised again and again by Shakespeare. Cassius's calculating practicality is in stark contrast to Brutus's impracticality. Cassius says, "Let *Antony* and *Caesar* fall together" and Brutus replies, "Let's be Sacrificers, but not Butchers *Caius*." Cassius is right but Brutus is the more human. Later, after the assassination, Brutus says of Antony, "I know that we shall have him well to Friend", and Cassius, right again, replies,

> my misgiving still
> Falles shrewdly to the purpose.
> [III. I. 146–7]

Brutus commits simple, fundamental errors of political tactics. The first is to invite Antony to speak at all at Caesar's funeral, then, having done so, to allow him to have last voice. The emergence of Antony as a leading character in the play serves, among other things, to underline Brutus's *naïveté*. Antony is a natural politician. The difference between his and Brutus's handling of the funeral speeches is immense. Brutus indulges in rhetoric—we feel that speech-making (certainly to a mob) is not his forte—and in idealism.

> Romans, Countrey-men, and Lovers, heare mee for my
> cause, and be silent, that you may heare. Beleeve me for

mine Honor, and have respect to mine Honor, that you may
beleeve.

[III. II. 13–17]

Antony manipulates his audience as if they were puppets, making
most of his points succinctly but never failing to labour the one
theme he knows will appeal to the acquisitive appetites of his
listeners—the contents of Caesar's will. He is completely aware of
what he does,

> Mischeefe thou art a-foot,
> Take thou what course thou wilt.

[III. II. 261–2]

and, like Octavius Caesar, is ruthless and Machiavellian.

The relationship between Octavius and Antony is based
entirely on expediency. They are both amoral. Their relationship
is in marked contrast to that which develops between Brutus and
Cassius and reaches fulfilment in Act Five. In the end it is, indeed,
as if Cassius, the shrewd politician, who in the early scenes gave
evidence of knowing the price of everything and the value of
nothing, is "tamed" into more human responses through his
friendship with Brutus. There is an acute dramatic irony in the
fact that Cassius, who rightly describes himself as "older in
practice" than Brutus, should accede to Brutus's decision (the
wrong one, typically) about the battle-plan. Cassius is practical,

> 'Tis better that the Enemie seeke us,
> So shall he waste his meanes, weary his Souldiers,
> Doing himself offence, whil'st we lying still,
> Are full of rest, defence, and nimblenesse.

[IV. III. 198–200]

but Brutus bases even his battle-plan upon abstraction,

> The Enemy encreaseth every day,
> We at the height, are readie to decline.
> There is a Tide in the affayres of men,
> Which taken at the Flood, leades on to Fortune:

[IV. III. 214–17]

These are worthy sentiments, but battles are won by shrewd plans not noble words. Yet Brutus persuades Cassius. What we witness in the emotionally charged scenes between Cassius and Brutus before Philippi is, it may be suggested, the conversion of a political man by a man of intellectual and emotional sensitivity. Cassius discovers what humanity means. It is difficult to avoid reflection upon a possible, if theoretical, similarity between these two men and Hamlet and Horatio. The latter is the more practical and, we infer, the more "political". It is Horatio who feels and expresses impatience at Hamlet's over-inquiring mind in the scene with gravediggers. Yet he lives to become Hamlet's final comforter. It is as if he finds love, as Cassius does, through his introspective, vulnerable, sensitive friend. Cassius's conversion is signalled in a speech he makes in Act Four, scene three.

> Come *Antony*, and yong *Octavius* come,
> Revenge your selves alone on *Cassius*,
> For *Cassius* is a-weary of the World:
> > [IV. III. 92–4]

He continues, a little later,

> Have not you love enough to beare with me,
> When that rash humour which my Mother gave me
> Makes me forgetfull.
> > [IV. III. 117–19]

No other play of Shakespeare's has such a valedictory atmosphere as has *Julius Caesar* in its final act. Foreboding, resignation and death are in the air. The discovered love between the once entirely political man and Brutus makes the very enterprise on which they are embarked seem irrelevant. Victory or defeat seems less important than that Brutus and Cassius have found love and respect for each other; Portia's death is of greater moment to Cassius than discussions about tactics and strategy. It seems more apt that Cassius and Brutus should part well and lovingly than that Brutus "gave the word too early" and ensured defeat for his army. Cassius makes no response to this revelation—his thoughts and feelings seem already to have left this world.

The relationship between these two men comes to dominate the last act of the play, and it ends leaving us with more of a feeling of having seen a personal than a social tragedy—we are less concerned about Rome and its future than with the sad fact of the untimely deaths of two noble Romans.

Yet, up to this last act, *Julius Caesar* is less concerned with individual tragedy than with a vividly naturalistic evocation of historical events whose meaning is still deeply embedded in the historical consciousness of Western Europe. Shakespeare's ability to give a present-tense actuality to those events is proven in several scenes—in Act One, scene one, where Flavius and Marullus berate the common citizenry, in Act Two, scene one, where Brutus greets and talks to the conspirators, and in the following scene, where we see Caesar in his domestic habitat before departing for the Capitol.

There is one such scene of vivid actuality which is remarkable for other reasons. It is Act Three, scene three, in which the poet Cinna is massacred by the Roman mob. It is not difficult, with Cinna's opening words in our minds, to imagine the fiery glow of burning property with, perhaps, a context of sultry thunder and vivid lightning.

> I dreamt to night, that I did feast with *Caesar*,
> And things unluckily charge my Fantasie:
> > [III. III. 1–2]

The brutality of the scene, achieved with such economy, attaches itself inexorably to the imagination. It is, in one sense, one painful minor event in a day full of important and unimportant happenings. It is often cut by theatre directors because they consider it superfluous. It is claimed that we already know that this Roman mob is dangerous and brutal and that, anyway, the death of an obscure, frightened poet is of little dramatic consequence. Such argument ignores the fact that the scene is a clear example of Shakespeare's superb sense of thematic and theatrical values. Shakespeare realised what, so often, his modern directors fail to grasp—that the brutal reality of mindless killing is best conveyed to an audience not when groups confront other groups with physical violence but when a single individual is menaced by a group. The death of Hector in *Troilus and Cressida*, of York in *Henry VI* and of Cinna in this play, are ample testimony. The doomed individual takes on a terrible vulnerability and becomes representative of all threatened men; his loneliness in the face of calculated death makes its vicious cruelty all the keener.

In the particular instance of Cinna the poet, another sensitivity of Shakespeare's is revealed. One of the first victims of social anarchy is a society's culture. Hitler's burning of the books, the activities of the so-called Red Guards in Maoist China, are evidence enough that what unreason fears first is the reason, order, and imaginative and intellectual freedom represented by art and culture. This Roman mob which, in any case, probably cannot read, is prepared to "tear" Cinna for "his bad verses". It is greater evidence of the rule of anarchy when even minor poets are killed.

And, finally, as one further testimony to the utter foolhardiness of cutting this scene, one can turn their own arguments against those modern directors who slavishly try "to make Shakespeare speak to the twentieth century" and upon this policy would delete the scene as being of no interest to a contemporary audience. William Shirer in his book *The Rise and Fall of the Third Reich*[5] recounts the story of Willi Schmidt, a minor musician, whose flat was invaded one evening in the 1930s by a group of Hitler's thugs while Schmidt and his family were having a musical evening among themselves; they inquired his name, and the last that his wife ever saw or heard of her husband was as he was brutally pushed downstairs he cried that he was not Willi Schmidt the politician, but Schmidt the musician. Across the centuries poor blubbering Cinna's cries are echoed in the words of another victim—"I am *Cinna* the Poet". We are reminded that what was true for Imperial Rome was true for Hitler's Germany and is true for us now.

This returns us to the most obvious quality of *Julius Caesar*—its innate ability to be "contemporary". Shakespeare's sense of politics, of man in society, of the tension between personal sensibility and public necessity, is so accurate that what he communicates in this play is an eternal reflection of the ironies, cruelties, and pains which man suffers in a politically organised society as he tries to reconcile what are probably irreconcilable—private and public morality, wisdom, and sensibility.

REFERENCES

Chapter 1

1. Waldo Clarke (ed.), *In Praise of Shakespeare*, 1949, p. 16.
2. See Bernard Beckermann, *Shakespeare at the Globe*, 1962.
3. G. E. Bentley, *Shakespeare: A Biographical Handbook*, 1961, p. 73.
4. *Ibid.*, p. 74.
5. *Ibid.*, pp. 99–100.
6. F. E. Halliday, *A Shakespeare Companion*, 1952, p. 237.
7. Bentley, pp. 106–7.
8. Beckermann, p. xiii.
9. Simon Forman (1552–1611). A schoolmaster, then astrologer, then medical quack, Forman frequently fell foul of the law though "protected" by a number of influential court ladies to whom he prescribed love potions and offered amatory advice. Among his many papers is *The Bocke of Plaies* containing notes on visits he paid to performances of *Macbeth*, *The Winter's Tale* and *Cymbeline*.
10. *Every Man Out of his Humour*, pub. 1600; *Sejanus*, pub. 1605; *Volpone*, pub. 1607.
11. Ascribed to Cyril Tourneur (d. 1626), but published anonymously in 1607.
12. Shakespeare probably acted in Jonson's *Every Man in his Humour*.
13. These references to Shakespeare from Jonson's works are conveniently identified in E. K. Chambers and C. Williams, *A Short Life of Shakespeare*, 1933, pp. 198–205.
14. *Ibid.*, p. 200.
15. See *The Apologie for Poetrie*, written *c.* 1580–82.
16. See John Dryden, *An Essay of Dramtick Poesie*, 1662. Both Sidney's essay (ref. 15) and Dryden's are published in

E. D. Jones (ed.), *English Critical Essays, XVI–XVIII centuries* (World's Classics), 1941.

17. See Thomas Fuller (1608–61), *Worthies of England*, 1662.

18. Robert Greene (1558–92). Poet, pamphleteer, polemicist, playwright, novelist and hack. His best works are *James IV* (*c.* 1591) and *Friar Bacon and Friar Bungay* (*c.* 1591). In *Groat's-worth of Wit* (1592) he attacks one called "Shake-scene" as "an upstart Crow, beautified with our feathers, that with his *Tygers hart wrapt in a Players hyde*, supposes he is as well able to bombast out a blanke verse as the best of you". This has been taken to be (and almost certainly is) a reference to Shakespeare—the only derogatory one that has come down to us.

19. Bentley, p. 36. The deed records an agreement between Shakespeare and William Underhill for "a messuage with two barns and two gardens with appurtenances".

20. *Ibid.*, p. 37.

21. *Ibid.*, pp. 37–8.

22. *Ibid.*, p. 38.

CHAPTER 2

1. Bandello (*c.* 1480–1562). His *Novelle* were published between 1554 and 1573. They consisted of 214 prose romances, and were translated from the original Italian into French by Belleforest (1530–83) as *Histoires Tragiques* (1559–82). Ariosto (1474–1533) first published *Orlando Furioso* in 1516; it was translated into English by Sir John Harington in 1591. Ariosto's work was one source for Spenser's *The Faerie Queene*, where Shakespeare may well have consulted a version of the same story in Book II, Canto IV.

2. G. Trenery (ed.), *Much Ado About Nothing*, Arden Edition, 1924, p. xxvi.

3. R. A. Foakes (ed.), *Much Ado About Nothing*, New Penguin Shakespeare, 1968, p. 25.

4. John Russell Brown, *Shakespeare and His Comedies*, 1957, p. 118.

5. Foakes, p. 16.

6. *Ibid.*, p. 20.

7. O. J. Campbell and E. G. Quinn (eds.), *A Shakespeare Encyclo-paedia*, 1966, p. 564.

8. T. J. B. Spencer (ed.), *Elizabethan Love Stories*, Penguin Shakespeare Library, 1968, pp. 11–12.

9. Anthony Munday (1553–1633). The play written in 1598.

10. Henry Chettle (1560–1607). His hand has also been identified in the MS. of *Sir Thomas More*—an MS. in which Shakespeare's hand is seen by some scholars.

11. Thomas Lodge (*c.* 1558–1625). *Rosalynde* was printed in 1590.

12. Robert Armin (d. 1615). Member of the Lord Chamberlain's company from 1599. Played Touchstone, Feste and Lear's Fool. Author of *Quips upon Questions* (1599); *Foole upon Foole, or Six Sortes of Sottes* (1600); *A Nest of Ninnies* (1608); *Phantasie, the Italian Tailor and his Boy* (1609).

13. See R. H. Goldsmith, *Wise Fools in Shakespeare*, 1957.

14. See Helen Gardner's essay on the play in John Garrett (ed.), *More Talking of Shakespeare*, 1960.

15. Barrister of the Middle Temple (d. 1622). His diary was edited for the Camden Society, 1868.

16. See Leslie Hotson, *The First Night of Twelfth Night*, 1954.

17. Comedy, acted originally in Sienna in 1531, but first published in 1537.

18. Included in Riche's *Riche his Farewell to Militarie Profession conteining verie pleasaunt discourse fit for a peacable tyme*, 1581.

19. See reference 1.

20. Spencer, p. 97.

21. See Hotson, *passim*, for the identification of Knollys and Malvolio.

22. Enid Welsford, *The Fool, his social and literary history*, 1935.

23. *Ibid.*, p. 168.

24. Goldsmith, p. 103.

25. Welsford, p. 30.

26. *Ibid.*, p. 199.

27. *As You Like It*, II. VII. 44–61.

CHAPTER 3

1. K. Muir (ed.), *Shakespeare, The Comedies*, 1965, p. 9.

2. William Empson, *The Structure of Complex Words*, 1951, p. 284.

3. O. J. Campbell in *A Shakespeare Encyclopaedia*, p. 136.

4. G. K. Hunter (ed.), *All's Well That Ends Well*, Arden Shakespeare, 1959, p. xxiii.

5. *Shakespeare, The Comedies*, p. 118.

6. Hunter, p. xlii.

7. See *Shakespeare, The Comedies*, pp. 135–51 for G. Wilson Knight's discussion of Helena as the supreme development of Shakespeare's idea of love as a "miracle-worker".

8. *Ibid.*, p. 138.

9. *Ibid.*, pp. 142–3.

10. Hunter, pp. xxxi–xxxii.

11. *Ibid.*, p. xliv.

12. *Ibid.*, p. xlvi.

13. *Ibid.*, p. xxxv.

14. *Ibid.*, p. xxxvii.

15. W. W. Lawrence, *Shakespeare's Problem Comedies*, 1969, p. 94.

16. *Ibid.*, p. 102.

17. R. W. Chambers, *Man's Unconquerable Mind*, 1939, pp. 307–8.

18. T. M. Parrott, *Shakespearean Comedy*, 1949, pp. 347–55.

19. Quoted in E. Wilson (ed.), *Shaw on Shakespeare*, 1969, p. 144.

20. J. M. Nosworthy (ed.), *Measure for Measure*, New Penguin Shakespeare, 1969, p. 40.

21. Donald Lupton, *London and the Countrey carbonadoed*, 1632. Quoted in J. Dover Wilson, *Life in Shakespeare's England*, 1964, p. 143.

22. In Dryden's version (1679) Cressida kills herself to demonstrate her fidelity to Troilus.

23. At the Royal Shakespeare Theatre; and subsequently at the Aldwych in 1969.

24. J. Dover Wilson (ed.), *Troilus and Cressida*, New Cambridge Shakespeare, 1969, p. xv.

25. *Women Beware Women*, I. II. 49–50. The play was published in 1657—thirty years after Middleton's death.

26. E. M. W. Tillyard, *Shakespeare's Problem Plays*, 1957, p. 63.

27. *Ibid.*, p. 53.

CHAPTER 4

1. There is an interesting discussion of the Orson Welles modern-dress production (1937), in *Mary McCarthy's Theatre Chronicles, 1937–62*, 1962.

2. Platter's original accounts were in German. This excerpt is translated by E. K. Chambers. See Chambers and Williams, *A Short Life of Shakespeare*, p. 173.

3. For example, Frank Dunlop's production at the Nottingham Playhouse in 1962.

4. T. J. B. Spencer (ed.), *Shakespeare's Plutarch*, Penguin Shakespeare Library, 1968, p. 145.

5. William Shirer, *The Rise and Fall of the Third Reich*, 1960, chapter 3, *passim*.